AMAZING IS MY

SUPERPOWER

Our Autism journey continues

By Elogeia. Hadley

AMAZING IS MY SUPERPOWER.
Our Autism journey continues
by Elogeia Hadley, Author.
This publication provides accurate information
on the subject covered. It is sold with the
understanding that no legal, accounting, or
professional services are provided. For expert
assistance, consult a qualified professional.

Book cover designed by Diocelina Padilla Jr.
More info Contact: diocejrpadilla@gmail.com

Introduction

I wrote this book to share my family's experience with autism. My goal is to create a manual, rather than just a straightforward narrative, providing a step-by-step account of how we navigated what the DSM-5 describes as autism spectrum disorder (ASD).

My younger sister and my son both live with autism, which inspired me to title the book "Amazing is My Superpower." This title highlights the uniqueness and courage required to face the daily challenges that come with autism. I wanted to illustrate the impact autism has had on our lives and the lives of our family and friends.

In this book, I share our journey of acceptance and how we have overcome many fears and obstacles. Each day, as a family, we continue to grow and learn more about autism.

I hope this book helps someone else. Don't let autism or any challenge you face define you. What some may see as a disability could be your superpower!

Contents

Part 1: The Beginning

He was a child born to two young parents. It was a new and scary experience for us to be parents at such a young age. I had no idea what to expect when my oldest son was born. At the time, I was still living with my parents. When we met, we were 18 years old, and I was in college. We started dating, and things moved quickly. A year later, we became parents. We were young and naive, focused on love, yet unsure of what to do. But we figured it out as time went on. My daughter was born three years later, arriving right on time—literally to the date.

After starting my career as a medical office assistant, I moved to the suburbs of Chicago. A few years later, so did my parents. Life took over for us with work and school. Then, my mom got sick with cervical cancer and later passed away. My dad moved north with my sister not long after that. I was devastated. I took care of my mom the best I could, with help from a hospice nurse and my aunt, until her last day. I learned so much about caring for someone, especially a loved one. I understood what to look for and what questions to ask. I also discovered that not everyone has your best interests at heart.

To this day, I still find myself in denial, thinking about what I could have done better and questioning myself. If I could have had one more moment with her, I would have researched more and sought additional help. My denial was filled with "shoulda, coulda, woulda."

As time passed, I improved at accepting my mother's death. However, I will never forget all her troubles with medical professionals and insurance companies. They made fighting for her care incredibly difficult in so many ways. We kept working while taking care of my children and our home. Then, in 2002, we had another baby boy, our third child. His birth was amazing. Unlike the other two, the room was quiet and still; the only movement was from the doctor and the nurses. The obstetrician was a soft-spoken man who only spoke to give me instructions. The boy's dad and siblings were also silent, including his brother, who slept through the entire delivery.

He was the sweetest little brown baby, with deep dimples and a round face. His eyes were already slightly open, peeking at me. He let out a little cry to show he was okay and that his lungs were working. As they cleaned him off and took his weight and length, they planned to immunize him the following day. I felt he was ready for the world, and his curious eyes seemed to be looking for something. I named him Talib, which means "seeker of knowledge."

When we got home, I was excited about this little bundle of joy. My family joined in the celebration with visits and gifts. We watched him grow and gain weight as he was supposed to. After two weeks, we started the well-baby checks, ensuring he was thriving and ready for his shots. And he was perfect!

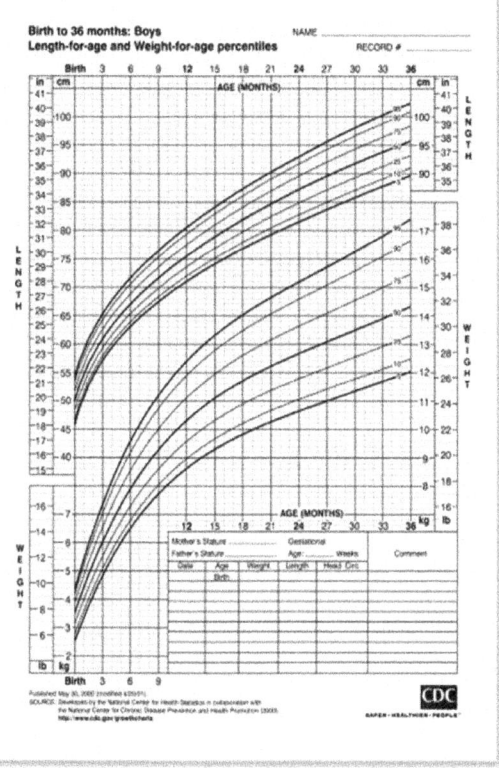

This form can be found on the Centers for Disease Control and Prevention (CDC) website.

One day, while I was at home taking care of my children, I noticed that I was having difficulty breathing. Feeling uneasy about my condition, especially as a new mom, I decided to go to the hospital.

7

Home alone with my infants and small children, I called my neighbor to take me to the ER. When I arrived at the hospital, the triage nurse, whom I knew, asked me if I had high blood pressure. I informed her that I didn't, but my family has a history of it. She gave me a worried look. When I asked her what my blood pressure was, she turned the machine around so I could see it. It was the highest it had ever been—around 189/110.

The nurse took me to the next room, alerted the ER physician, and immediately informed me that if I were nursing, I would have to stop because the medication they needed to give me could harm the baby.

The hospital conducted several blood tests, a chest x-ray, and an echocardiogram, and diagnosed me with bilateral pneumonia, which involved fluid around my heart. As a result, I had to stop nursing and call my family for help with my baby and the other children, as well as their father. We also recruited my cousins to assist me, since I needed to transition my baby's feedings from nursing to powdered milk, and I was too weak to manage everything on my own.

See the reference page for more information about verywell

After almost a week in the hospital, I returned home to care for my little family. Life continued with my new bundle of joy. About three years later, I had my last child, a daughter, and faced a similar situation. This time, I was diagnosed with bilateral pneumonia, along with some issues related to the left ventricle of my heart. Here I was, a young mother of four, extremely sick and fighting for my life. It was suggested that, due to my heart condition, I should consider not having any more children, so I decided to undergo tubal ligation. Despite everything, our little family persevered.

Part 2: Bird Calls and the Silver Spoon

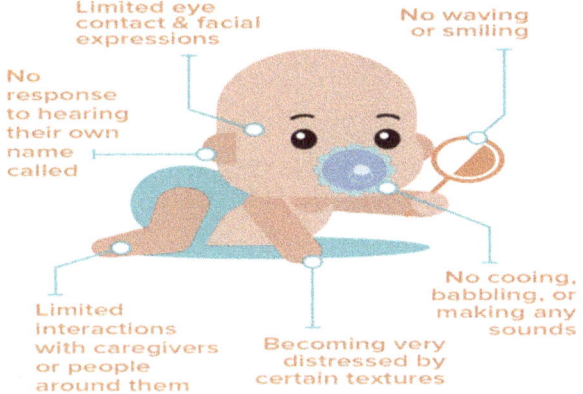

SIGNS OF AUTISM
IN BABIES AND TODDLERS

Limited eye contact & facial expressions

No waving or smiling

No response to hearing their own name called

No cooing, babbling, or making any sounds

Limited interactions with caregivers or people around them

Becoming very distressed by certain textures

By the time he was 8 months old, he had become a highly active and rambunctious baby. He crawled through the house, played with his toys and siblings, and pulled himself up in an attempt to walk. He was a good sleeper and rarely woke up during the night.

One night, while we were sleeping, I heard a strange noise coming from his crib. It was a weak, squeaky sound, almost like an injured bird. I sat up in bed, got out, and walked over to check on him, but nothing was there except him sleeping peacefully. I had never heard a baby make that sound before. He made the noise a few more times, but it did not bother him.

During his 18- to 20-month well-child check, everything went great. He was healthy and growing well. I asked the pediatrician about the strange sounds, but he seemed puzzled. His expression said it all: "This lady is crazy, but I'll entertain her." He asked me what the sound was like, but I struggled to replicate it accurately.

The doctor reassured me, saying, "Well, he is a healthy baby and will be getting his immunizations today." And he did; he didn't cry when the nurse administered the shots in his thighs. Instead, he stared at her hands and looked at me for approval. I smiled and gave him a "you are doing so great" smile.

At the end of the visit, the doctor reviewed the growth and development chart and asked if he was saying any words or forming complete sentences. He wasn't just making those bird-like sounds, babbling, and doing much pointing, but not much actual talking.

I didn't think much of it until the next visit. The pediatrician informed me that he should be saying more words and forming sentences, at least enough to ask for food or express his wants. Since he wasn't, the pediatrician suggested that he might have a speech delay. He recommended we learn some basic sign language and wrote a referral for a speech therapist.

Basic sign language for children with autism or speech delays can be beneficial.

PART 3: Tale of Two Therapists

We started speech therapy with two therapists, who were as different as night and day. The older therapist arrived, assessed him, and managed to get him to sit still long enough to complete the 40-minute session. The younger therapist, however, struggled to capture his attention; he would run circles around her. This toddler had us chasing him like we were children. He wasn't listening to us; he was running and laughing, which was embarrassing. I could see she was frustrated, and so were we. She had a look that seemed to say, "These people cannot control their child."

Later, we moved to a new district, and he had therapy in a half-day preschool for just a few minutes in the classroom. I also noticed that his attachment to certain toys had become almost obsessive, particularly those with spinning wheels. His number one toy was Thomas the Tank Engine. He would sit for hours, holding that little train and spinning its wheels. He had all the trains and the books, but he would set them aside; he only seemed to want the little train with the movable wheels. Whenever we passed train tracks or a bridge, he would scream "CHOO-CHOO!" and insist that everyone had to say it with him, like his background singers, or else he would have a meltdown. It was a comical car full of people forced to sing choo-choo train songs.

He also had an attachment to a large silver gravy spoon. We carried it just in case things become complicated. That spoon was his security and my sanity. His grip on that spoon was tight; he even held it while sleeping. At that point, we were using whatever worked to keep him calm. We thought he had a great sense of humor; he would play peek-a-boo, run circles around us, and laugh. However, there were moments when he would throw things at people, and we couldn't stop him. He didn't respond to time-outs or threats of "stop or else." He seemed oblivious to any discipline, and once again, we felt powerless.

I remember my daughter's sixth birthday party when he was 3 years old; he got out of control. He slapped several children, a few adults, and even a 6-month-old infant. I was so upset; we couldn't stop him. I even gave him a few swats on the butt just to get his attention, but he just laughed at me. It didn't intimidate him one bit. His energy level was exhausting. Eventually, the other children would simply sit aside and watch him because he would outrun and outplay any child on the playground. The party was over!

PART 4: Fearless Train Chaser

As school life progressed, we noticed differences in him compared to our other three children. He had a higher energy level and was overly friendly. He would approach strangers, talking and reaching out to them, often wandering off without fear. We thought, "Wow, this kid is fearless," until one incident during first-grade summer school changed our perspective on fearlessness.

A nearby train blew its horn while the children were outside for recess. He took off joyfully, running toward the train, believing it was a larger version of Thomas the Tank Engine. The teacher mentioned that she had to run as fast as she could to catch him. This incident was a wake-up call for us; something was happening that we couldn't quite understand, and it was unlike anything we had experienced with our other children. It wasn't very comforting. The teacher said he had no fear; even when she grabbed and tackled him, he just laughed.

As a few years passed, nothing changed. He still exhibited no fear of people or animals, lacking the "stranger danger" instinct that most children have. I began paying more attention to him and noticed more differences than my other children and his peers. The children around him were using more words and speaking in complete sentences. It seemed they were progressing faster than he was cognitively, and he struggled to keep up with his peers in many ways, which concerned us.

PART 5: The Meltdown

DID YOU KNOW?

Autism Awareness Facts by www.theautismdad.com

Autism

Autism is easily among the most misunderstood of all the human conditions.

Among the most misunderstood things about Autism is the "meltdown".

Meltdowns

- Are NOT a disciplinary problem
- Are NOT an indication of bad parenting
- Are NOT an indication of a misbehaving child
- Are NOT within the childs control

- ARE a result of overstimulation
- ARE the body's way of purging
- ARE very common in people with Autism
- ARE easily confused with tantrums

I remember the meltdowns. They were different from tantrums because nothing could quiet or satisfy him. They were full-on meltdowns to the point where I had to leave the store because I couldn't get anything done, nor could I calm him down. In those days, even the silver spoon didn't help.

I recall going to the department store with my cousin while she was shopping for a special occasion. We had been in the store for about 30 minutes when the full-on meltdown began—there were no warnings. It was more than just crying; it involved flailing arms, stiffening up, screaming, kicking, and holding him. I took a deep breath, feeling lost and unsure of what to do. Tears streamed down my face as I ran out of the store, aware of the people staring at me as if I had done something wrong. My cousin followed closely behind, her expression a mix of disbelief and confusion. She tried to comfort me, but nothing seemed to help. When we got home, I was utterly exhausted and overwhelmed. I felt powerless as a mother. I kept asking myself, "What is wrong with my baby?" The pediatrician explained that the tantrums resulted from my child's inability to communicate effectively. However, it felt like more than just poor communication; it seemed to be something more profound.

The doctor warned me that we should be prepared for the possibility that he may not speak or communicate at all; this might be our reality. I was crushed and devastated. Was this real? Was this all for us? No other options? I questioned, "What did I do wrong?" and "Did I cause this?" A flood of questions rushed through my mind. What role had I played in making him this way? I realized my baby would need exceptional help, but I didn't know where to start.

PART 6: Happy Go-Lucky!

EAT DRINK MORE

At 4 years old, he is more outgoing, happier, and always smiling and playing. He rarely seems upset about anything and doesn't cry much anymore, except for occasional meltdowns, which have now become rare. We learned enough sign language to help him communicate. He would ask and answer questions such as whether he was hungry, if he wanted to eat, if he wanted more, or if he wanted to play. Learning the basics of toddler sign language has helped him begin speaking a little more. We have noticed that he is still delayed in forming complete sentences, but we are doing our best to support him at home, and the schools are also contributing to his therapies.

PART 7: Phone Calls and Letters

As time passed, the issue with the teachers persisted for a few years. Phone calls and letters became more frequent, complaining that he would not sit still, constantly moving around the classroom, and frequently visiting and disturbing other children during class time. Of course, we mentioned this to our pediatrician. After a series of new tests for him and questions for both us and the teachers, who were also required to answer the same set of questions in a questionnaire, he was diagnosed with attention deficit hyperactivity disorder (ADHD) and speech and language delays.

I had recently heard of ADHD, but it was not a diagnosis in my generation, so I had doubts. This was all new to us; we saw him as a highly active toddler. I guess we were a little skeptical.

It was also suggested that he be placed in an Individualized Education Program (IEP) since he had fallen significantly behind in school. This would allow him to receive the necessary therapies. The pediatrician, the same one who suggested my child might not talk, recommended medication as the only treatment. My maternal instincts were raised! It seemed to me that nobody had a solid idea of what was happening or why medication was seen as the answer. He also mentioned an immunization for human papillomavirus (HPV), and we received the first shot in the office that day.

This was news to me. As a former medical assistant who had worked with physicians for years, I remembered them telling patients that medication is not always the answer; many times, lifestyle changes can be effective. I also did not recall them being so eager to prescribe medication to a small child. Shouldn't it be the last resort?

We went back to the pediatrician for another well-child visit and started a new ADHD medication that the doctor recommended. This one caused my son's stomach aches, and he rapidly lost weight. He was often doubled over in pain at night. When we informed the pediatrician, the recommendation was to lower the dosage, but that did not help. We then switched to another medication that the doctor recommended. This one "worked" in that it slowed him down, but he could not sleep at night.

We kept informing the pediatrician that nothing was working, and we were not willing to watch him endure the side effects any longer. The suggestion was to keep changing the medications until we found one that was a "good fit," as if we were trying on shoes. This cannot be good. At this point, I honestly did not know what to do.

PART 8: And the Beat Goes On!

No medications seemed to work for him to my satisfaction. As the daughter of a natural healer and a former medical professional, I knew that all this medication would likely have some long-term side effects. It also harmed him more than it helped. Instead of improving his condition, it made Talib feel like a zombie and caused headaches, stomach aches, and other issues.

In dealing with his problems, I began to feel sick myself. I felt weak and fatigued and started to break out in rashes. After a visit to my doctor, I was diagnosed with discoid lupus erythematosus, an autoimmune disease that affects my skin, bones, and hair. So now, not only did I have to figure out his issues, but I also had to address my own.

This led me to explore alternative ways of living. I began researching more effective methods to calm him down, focusing on one symptom at a time. I understood that it would take time and that nothing happened overnight. All I knew was not to give up and to keep going, taking it one day at a time.

PART 9: Tag, You're It!

As school life progressed, the teachers continued to complain, regardless of whether he was on medication or not. Now that we have moved up a few grades, the complaints have shifted to him sitting too close to other kids, talking out of turn, and not understanding boundaries. One significant incident occurred in fourth grade during a game called "Tag." He didn't quite understand the rules or how to play. No one explained the game to him; it was assumed he knew what to do.

An email from the teacher stated, "He put another child in a chokehold today during playtime." There was talk of a suspension, but after investigating the situation, the teacher concluded that my son didn't understand the game. When the other child tagged him, he thought it was an intentional hit or punch and began to defend himself.

This situation raised concerns about testing him for something else, but that never happened. Instead, we continued to search for better ways to accommodate him, including adjusting his medication.

CHILD STUDY CENTER
Department of Pediatrics
University of Oklahoma Health Sciences Center

Vanderbilt ADHD Diagnostic Parent Rating Scale

Parent's Name: _____ Today's Date: _____ Child's Name: _____ Age: ____

Directions: Each rating should be considered in the context of what is appropriate for the age of your child and should reflect that child's behavior in the last 6 months.

Is this evaluation based on a time when the child   was on medication   was not on medication   not sure?

BEHAVIOR:	never	occasionally	often	very often
1. Does not pay attention to details or makes careless mistakes; for example, homework.	0	1	2	3
2. Has difficulty attending to what needs to be done.	0	1	2	3
3. Does not seem to listen when spoken to directly.	0	1	2	3
4. Does not follow through when given directions and fails to finish things.	0	1	2	3
5. Has difficulty organizing tasks and activities.	0	1	2	3
6. Avoids, dislikes, or does not want to start tasks that require ongoing mental effort.	0	1	2	3
7. Loses things needed for tasks or activities (assignments, pencils, or books).	0	1	2	3
8. Is easily distracted by noises or other things.	0	1	2	3
9. Is forgetful in daily activities.	0	1	2	3
10. Fidgets with hands or feet or squirms in seat.	0	1	2	3
11. Leaves seat when he/she is supposed to stay in his/her seat.	0	1	2	3
12. Runs about or climbs too much when he/she is supposed to stay seated.	0	1	2	3
13. Has difficulty playing or starting quiet games.	0	1	2	3
14. Is "on the go" or often acts as if "driven by a motor".	0	1	2	3
15. Talks too much.	0	1	2	3
16. Blurts out answers before questions have been completed.	0	1	2	3
17. Has difficulty waiting for his/her turn.	0	1	2	3
18. Interrupts or bothers others when they are talking or playing games.	0	1	2	3
19. Argues with adults.	0	1	2	3
20. Loses temper.	0	1	2	3
21. Actively disobeys or refuses to follow an adult's requests or rules.	0	1	2	3
22. Bothers people on purpose.	0	1	2	3
23. Blames others for his/her mistakes or misbehaviors.	0	1	2	3
24. Is touchy or easily annoyed by others.	0	1	2	3
25. Is angry or bitter.	0	1	2	3
26. Is hateful and wants to get even.	0	1	2	3
27. Bullies, threatens, or scares others.	0	1	2	3
28. Starts physical fights.	0	1	2	3
29. Lies to get out of trouble or to avoid jobs (i.e., "cons" others).	0	1	2	3
30. Skips school without permission.	0	1	2	3
31. Is physically unkind to people.	0	1	2	3
32. Has stolen things that have value.	0	1	2	3
33. Destroys others' property on purpose.	0	1	2	3
34. Is physically mean to animals.	0	1	2	3
35. Has set fires on purpose to cause damage.	0	1	2	3
36. Has broken into someone else's home, business or car.	0	1	2	3
37. Has stayed out at night without permission.	0	1	2	3
38. Has run away from home overnight.	0	1	2	3
39. Is fearful, anxious, or worried.	0	1	2	3
40. Is afraid to try new things for fear of making mistakes.	0	1	2	3
41. Feels useless or inferior.	0	1	2	3
42. Blames self for problems, feels at fault.	0	1	2	3
43. Feels lonely, unwanted, or unloved; complains that "no one loves him/her".	0	1	2	3
44. Is sad, unhappy, or depressed.	0	1	2	3
45. Feels different and easily embarrassed.	0	1	2	3

PERFORMANCE: How is your child doing?	Excellent	Above Average	Average	Somewhat of a Problem	Problematic
1. Rate how your child is doing in school overall.	1	2	3	4	5
2. How is your child doing in reading?	1	2	3	4	5
3. How is your child doing in writing?	1	2	3	4	5
4. How is your child doing in math?	1	2	3	4	5
5. How does your child get along with you?	1	2	3	4	5
6. How does your child get along with brothers and sisters?	1	2	3	4	5
7. How does your child get along with others his/her own age?	1	2	3	4	5
8. How does your child do in activities such as games or team play?	1	2	3	4	5

If more than six items from questions 1 - 9 or 10 - 18 are rated 2 or 3,
how old was your child when you first noticed these behaviors?

PART 10: The Negotiator!

We began a new journey, frequently seeking medication and the advice of various physicians and specialists in hopes of finding better help for him. I found myself driving 30 miles from home in search of assistance because things were only worsening for him in junior high school. The bullying and teasing had started, and he began responding physically.

We instructed him to find a teacher if he was being bullied and to come home to report it to us. However, he often didn't make it home before we received a phone call to pick him up due to another incident. He had been informing the teachers about the bullying, but nothing was being done to resolve the situation. He felt he needed to "defend himself, and when he did, he faced suspension for participating in a fight.

I struggled to understand the rules. It seemed acceptable for other children to taunt and bully him, but when the victims fought back, they faced the consequences, not the bullies. That old-school way of defending oneself against bullies is no longer tolerated in schools. Instead, they expect students to lie in a fetal position and brace for impact.

As we sat at the table with the principal, the dean, and the hall monitor—who turned out to be an off-duty police officer I hadn't invited—the conversation centered on why my son had been suspended for 10 days due to the fight. I firmly stated, "No! He is a special needs student!" I questioned why the school had not addressed the issues beforehand, rather than allowing them to escalate to this point.

"Why didn't they call to inform us that he was being bullied or had an issue?" I asked. She pushed a paper across the table stating that the school policy does not tolerate fighting and that he must be suspended. I pushed the paper back to her and told her that it was ridiculous to have a special needs child out of school for that long. What was the point of education if the child was not in school?

I had grown tired of this back-and-forth, suspension after suspension. It felt pointless! Why do we have an IEP (Individualized Education Program) in place for a special needs child without exceptional help or treatment? At this point, he might as well be an average child without the IEP. So, I repeated, "No suspension." They returned with a proposal for six days out of school, and again, I said no.

"Well, how about two days in school and three days out?" they countered. I replied, "Wow, now we're negotiating, and I guess I don't have a choice." I told them, "Your policy is ridiculous for these special needs children. What are they learning when they are consistently being suspended and excluded from school? I am frustrated because no one is showing any concern about the bullying, suspensions, or my child's future."

I felt he should have had exceptional circumstances, not constant suspensions, because he had special needs. I sensed that this was happening to him because he is African American. After all, I knew this wasn't happening to white children with similar disabilities; they were not being suspended in the same way. For some reason, they are seen as just having a "bad day," so why can't my son have one too?

I have seen it with my own eyes: Black children are often viewed as troublemakers, regardless of whether they have a disability. Why can't people feel sympathy for him? Something is happening, and I am desperate for support.

I suspected that the school viewed these suspensions as a way to reduce the number of Black students. So, I decided to speak with the dean. During our conversation, she mentioned that she had a sister with Down syndrome. I asked her, "Would you suspend your special-needs sister if she were trying to defend herself?"

She didn't respond verbally, but her expression and body language conveyed everything I needed to know. Of course, she wouldn't—she would never suspend her sister. I took this as a clear 'no.' I then asked her why my son was being suspended when he was merely defending himself and had unique needs. By that time, I was so distraught that I could feel their eyes watching me lose control. I couldn't hold back the tears, and to make matters worse, the off-duty police officer was annoyed with me. With one big huff, he folded his arms and rolled his eyes. That was it; I lost it. All the professionalism I was desperately clinging to went out the window. I asked him to leave the room, telling him he wasn't invited in the first place. This was all too much for me to understand or process. Why would they keep suspending a child with special needs? At that moment, I felt he was being treated like a criminal.

He was now officially seen as the bad kid, the problem child, the troublemaker. Year after year, the suspensions continued, and it seemed like the medication was making things worse. No matter what he did, people would label him as "the bad kid" or "the troublemaker." It was unfortunate because none of it was true. He was just a good kid in need of some extra attention and someone who cared.

Over time, the other kids realized that he was an easy target to blame. They began teasing and provoking him, understanding that he desperately wanted friendship. One girl even pretended to be his girlfriend before setting him up to be bullied on social media. They all laughed at him for being different. My heart broke for him because I didn't realize how cruel children—and some adults—could be.

After fight after fight and suspension after suspension, I finally said, "Enough is enough." I pulled him out of school and homeschooled him for the rest of the year. Feeling mentally drained, I reached out to friends and family for advice and guidance.

Part 11: The Cry for Help!

I decided to reach out on social media because I knew there would be someone to help us. We were mentally and emotionally spiraling out of control, and it was painful for me to watch him go through such suffering. Finally, I received some notifications on my Messenger. A few old high school classmates, all educators, reached out with helpful information. My childhood friend Barbara called and reassured me that my feelings were valid. She had worked as a teacher's assistant for Easter Seals before retiring and offered me some eye-opening advice and support. Many people responded to my cry for help, and I felt a sense of relief.

There was one person who reached out to me that I had never met before, but at that point, I was desperate and thought that if she could help, it wouldn't matter. Let us call her T. She felt terrible about what my family was going through with my son and said, "You're not the only person facing this; you're not alone, because I see this all the time." She mentioned that she had just spoken to a few other parents experiencing similar issues and told me about a group of student attorneys who could assist me for free with my situation.

I spoke to her for a while and discovered that she is a mom and a teacher in the south suburbs of Chicago. She asked if my son had an I.E.P. (Individual Education Program). I confirmed that he did. Then she asked what I wanted to do. I wasn't sure at the time, but I explained that the school kept suspending him for defending himself, and he was also being bullied; yet, no one seemed to care or take action.

She informed me that children with disabilities are protected under Illinois law, and all school districts are required to comply with these regulations. She provided me with a phone number for child advocacy and urged me to contact her as soon as possible, which I did.

After a few weeks of discussing my concerns with my family and friends, many of whom are concerned educators who work with children with disabilities, they began to offer me advice. My best friend, Barbara, encouraged me to make a call. She mentioned that she has seen similar situations spiral out of control and that it seemed like he, like many other disabled children, was being targeted. This often happens, particularly when families are not paying close attention or may not fully understand the child's disabilities. She also emphasized the importance of being involved and familiarizing oneself with the teachers and school policies.

Following their advice, I contacted a child advocacy group, which referred me to a service closer to my area. I spoke with a young woman who took some personal information and asked me about the issues at his school. She wanted to know what I hoped to achieve from this conversation. I shared my concerns about the suspensions, the bullying, and how I felt that no one cared about how much school he was missing.

She instructed me not to inform the schools that we were in communication and offered to provide an escort to some of these meetings if needed. She also sent me printable information about the laws protecting children with disabilities. For the first time in years, I felt like I was being heard, and that someone truly understood what I was going through.

Part 12: A Rough Summer!

During the summer, while we were homeschooling, my son began to cry uncontrollably. No matter what I did, I couldn't console him. He had seen something on the internet that sent him into a complete breakdown. I made him something to eat and tried to calm him down, but he was convinced that the world was ending, and I couldn't change his mind.

It was quiet in the house, so I went to see where he was. I found him lying on the sofa in a fetal position, with a glassy look in his eyes. I told him the world was not ending, but he became angry and punched a hole in the wall. I decided to take him to the ER for an evaluation. I explained what was happening and what he was saying. They called in an intake person from behavioral health to talk to him.

They took away all his clothes, leaving only his underwear, and led us to a small room with nothing in it but a bed, a door, and a small window. I knew what this room was: the psych room, where they also placed patients dealing with alcohol issues and suicidal thoughts. I remember working in the ER as a registration clerk, collecting information from these individuals, often with judgment. Sometimes, I would overhear the nurses and doctors talking about them, shaming them, and even laughing at their situations.

Now, here I was on the other side of the door. It's not funny when it's someone you love. For the first time in my adult life and as a mother, I found myself completely at a loss. I didn't know how to react or what to do. You never know what the universe will teach you. It's best to listen and learn from it.

The nurses and doctors treated us distantly; they were not very friendly. Even getting a glass of water was a challenge. I approached the desk and said, "Excuse me," but no one answered. I know they saw me standing there, but I was ignored. I had to get their attention by being loud: "Excuse me! Excuse me! Can we get a cup of water?" They were slow to move and seemed irritated. When we finally received the water, it came with a stare of shame. Now, they would think we both had issues, but so what? Let them believe what they want. I was here concerned about my son; nothing else mattered then.

Finally, the intake social worker came to speak with me about my son's history and the reason I brought him for an evaluation. She then spoke with him without me in the room. After about 45 minutes, she came out of the locked room with a small window and said they would keep him for observation for six days. I called his dad, who was horrified at what I had done, but told him I didn't know what else to do. He wasn't there to see our boy's confused and terrified look as he punched the walls.

We met with the psychiatrist, the nurse, the other staff, and the supervisor to discuss his progress and aftercare. They informed us that they had noticed he had been hallucinating, not eating well, and not sleeping. The lack of sleep could contribute, as Taalib told them he was up all night and never really slept. The medication they were giving him for sleep was Benadryl, along with an antipsychotic called Seroquel. They wanted to keep him for the full six days, but at this point, his father intervened. He said, "No, we want him home; we can take care of him there." The doctor advised us to keep him for observation, but his father was adamant. We didn't know how this process worked but believed we could achieve the same results with the available resources.

I could feel the tension in the room. The staff members were stunned, and they were not happy about it. We asked if we could see my son for a few minutes to check on him. When he walked into the room, he was happy to see us, dressed in hospital scrubs and soft slippers, escorted by a security guard. We asked how he was doing, and he said he was "ready to go home" but felt better.

We had to explain to him that we could not take him home until the doctors said he was ready. After a few more hugs and kisses, he returned to his room. We followed him and found a stark brick room with white paint, bare walls, and a single bed with a few white sheets—nothing else. My heart sank. What had I done?

We returned to the main room to talk further with the team and staff. Once again, they insisted that my son should stay, and the debate resumed. His dad continued to insist that we take him home, but the doctor said that by law, they could keep him for further care. If that were the case, we would have to call the Department of Children and Family Services (DCFS)—a lump formed in my throat. The room felt hot, and I could feel myself going into a rage because I knew nothing good had ever come from DCFS. But I also knew I couldn't show my emotions. All my fears about losing my child started to flood my mind, so I did my best to remain calm. "I have to get through this," I thought to myself. His dad, however, was irritated and did not hold back his frustrations.

"Why would you do that? We are trying to take care of our son," Talib's father asked.

"You can call them if you want," I replied. That doesn't change my mind; my son is coming home. He is not staying here six days." There was more back-and-forth, but we stood our ground, insisting they couldn't keep him that long. Eventually, both sides calmed down, and we agreed he should stay at least two more days for observation, a few doses of medication, and to ensure he was sleeping well.

When his two days were up, I went to pick him up with some fresh clothes and shoes. I had a brief conversation with the staff to confirm his medication, and I was relieved to hear that he was finally sleeping through the night. They believed his sleep deprivation may have caused him to be hyper-focused and hallucinate. But he was better, and we were finally going home.

Before I left, a supervisor pulled me aside. She said she was impressed by how our family stood together. She shared that she had a 34-year-old daughter with special needs, and when her daughter was 12, her husband left her because he couldn't accept having a child with special needs. She hugged me and wished us good luck.

When we got home, Talib wanted some "real food," a home-cooked meal. We ate and discussed what had happened. We kept him on his medication, saw the recommended psychiatrist at the local county clinic due to insurance issues, and used that service temporarily until we could find another psychiatrist. However, the doctor there seemed uninvolved and nonchalant—she appeared too young, tired and burned out. It didn't feel very comforting, as they appeared there to write prescriptions.

Eventually, I could add him to my medical insurance through my employer, and we returned to our pediatrician while searching for a child psychiatrist. It took all I could manage, and I couldn't take it anymore.

After school ended and summer began, we decided to homeschool for the new year. However, I refused to let him go back to his previous school. We transferred him to another school in the district that appeared to be better, though not perfect. The principal was more supportive, there was a better team, and his grades were satisfactory, but he still struggled with concentration. Overall, things seem to be improving—so far, so good.

I took him to his pediatrician for a check-up and discussed everything happening with him. We talked about his hospitalization in the psychiatric unit and the challenges he faced in school. The doctor asked if we were getting our immunizations, and the flu shot during our visit.

I presented him with an immunization waiver to sign, but it seemed he didn't hear anything I said; he was focused solely on the immunizations. I insisted that we wouldn't be giving him any more vaccinations until we figured out what was going on with my son. No one could seem to provide a direct answer about his behavior. My other three children did not have these issues, so I didn't understand what was happening to my baby boy. I questioned whether these immunizations or medications would even help him. At that point, he had already received enough chemicals and antibodies in his system. I just wanted him to have a fresh start. He had had more vaccinations than I did at his age.

They didn't understand what it felt like to watch my son being mentally tortured. I could look into his eyes and see that he was trapped, and my intuition told me something wasn't right. This 70-year-old man looked at me as if I had committed a crime. He frowned and stomped around the office in frustration, declaring, "So, I take it you're not going to get his flu shot or Gardasil?" I couldn't believe my ears. He was completely ignoring me.

I looked at him and said, "NO." Before I could say another word, he stormed out of the room and didn't come back. His nurse came in and handed us our discharge papers. Attached was the unsigned immunization form; he had also refused to sign the waiver. He had received more shots than I had ever had as a child, yet his reaction was still very disappointing. This doctor had a tantrum in front of me and my children, acting like a toddler.

But now, I recognize this as a sign. I could see what he thought of me, but he didn't understand what we were going through. Until I could figure out what was happening with my son, no one was going to inject him with anything else. This was our choice, and we would have to live with it. I was willing to take a chance. If my children want vaccinations later in life, they can make that decision, but I have had enough of not getting the truth and being ignored and mistreated.

It was time to put on my boxing gloves and lace up my boots; it was time to fight. It was time for my son and my family to go to war. Enough is enough!

Part 13: More Doctors, More Problems

At the end of the school year, we hoped the next year would improve our situation. We continued with the doctor's visits and maintained the medication that was not working well. Not only was my son experiencing stomach issues, but he was also displaying a particularly manic personality, making him very unpredictable. We worked hard to find another psychiatrist to either change his medication or provide us with suggestions on how to proceed.

Around this time, I had begun my journey with lupus, trying to stay calm and avoid stress, which proved to be challenging. The situation with my son was incredibly stressful, making it difficult to remain positive.

Throughout my journey, I discovered ways to alleviate my pain and manage lupus flares by making better food choices and seeing my physicians regularly. I thought, why not introduce Talib to a different diet as well?

Perhaps it could help him with stomach aches, mainly since the gastroenterologist had not provided any solutions. He only suggested more medication. Not only did he have stomach pain because of his medication, but his bowel movements were already unusual; the unusual ones were round, softball-sized, and would stop up toilets. We were told it was because he was constipated, and this could be resolved with anti-constipation medicines. But that only made things worse for him.

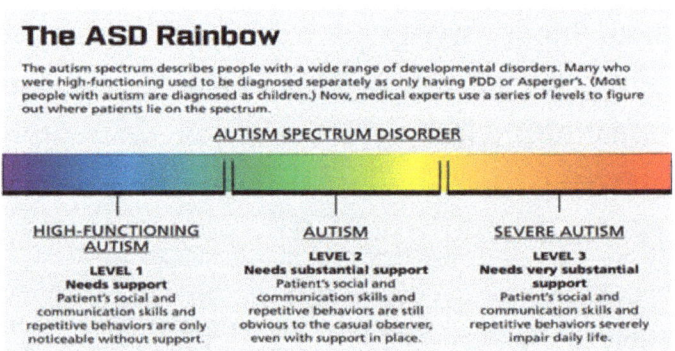

The ASD Rainbow

The autism spectrum describes people with a wide range of developmental disorders. Many who were high-functioning used to be diagnosed separately as only having PDD or Asperger's. (Most people with autism are diagnosed as children.) Now, medical experts use a series of levels to figure out where patients lie on the spectrum.

AUTISM SPECTRUM DISORDER

HIGH-FUNCTIONING AUTISM	AUTISM	SEVERE AUTISM
LEVEL 1	LEVEL 2	LEVEL 3
Needs support	Needs substantial support	Needs very substantial support
Patient's social and communication skills and repetitive behaviors are only noticeable without support.	Patient's social and communication skills and repetitive behaviors are still obvious to the casual observer, even with support in place.	Patient's social and communication skills and repetitive behaviors severely impair daily life.

Part 14: The Call

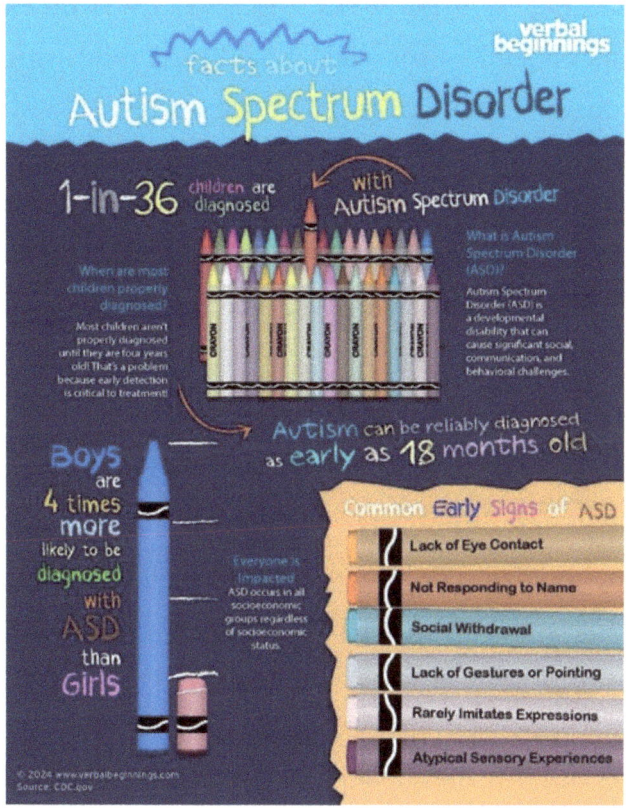

One day, I received a phone call from a medical center wanting to set up an appointment for additional psychological testing. I recalled my last appointment with a county health psychologist, where I expressed my concerns about a change in my son's behavior. I asked if further testing was necessary, and she agreed, mentioning that she suspected he might be on the autism spectrum but was not qualified to conduct such tests; her only role was to prescribe medication.

I scheduled the appointment, which was split into two days, each lasting approximately three hours. We arrived extremely late to the first appointment due to traffic, but they took the time to speak with us for a few minutes to understand our situation. They informed us that the behavioral health hospital had referred us. The second appointment lasted about two and a half hours: the first thirty minutes included both of us, followed by an individual session for me, and finally, just my son alone.

After the sessions, we were told it would take about a week to finalize everything. Less than a week later, a large envelope arrived with a diagnosis of intellectual disabilities, Autism Spectrum Disorder (ASD), restrictive and repetitive behavior (level 1), and social-communication disorder (level 2).

The suggestions and recommendations included several therapies and additional support systems both in and outside of school. However, I was left wondering why there was no mention of ADHD. Was my son misdiagnosed, or was his diagnosis presumed? All this time, we could have been helping him, and he could have received the therapies and support he needed since most children are diagnosed around the ages of 3 or 4. At least now, I have a more precise direction to follow. It shouldn't have taken this long, but I'm grateful we finally have answers.

Part 15: Less than 30 Minutes

Summer was here again, and I had to find a new pediatrician and arrange other therapies. Once again, I turned to social media for references. In the meantime, I temporarily visited my primary care physician while we searched for the right fit—someone knowledgeable about autism.

As summer was ending, I knew we had little time left. I found a pediatrician in Chicago who seemed promising. I made an appointment and spoke with her, and found that she was highly knowledgeable about ADD, ADHD, and autism. The appointment went well, and I even learned a few things I hadn't known before. For instance, I discovered that many children on the autism spectrum are often misdiagnosed at first because their lack of communication can lead to acting out. Additionally, many children on the spectrum don't do well with medication, as the core issues often relate to communication and social challenges. If you can address those two areas for a child on the spectrum, their outcomes and future can improve significantly.

She also recommended that we find a social group, a social worker, or a psychiatrist for him—someone who would be on our side and at least give us the benefit of the doubt.

I began searching for African American doctors for cultural reasons and to help manage medication refills. We found a psychiatrist near my home, so we made an appointment. The office was like all the others—nothing special. Talib and I went in together, and the doctor introduced himself and spoke for about ten minutes. Then, he wanted to separate us to talk to Taalib alone, so I sat outside in the waiting area for about 20 minutes.

When he called me back in, he said, "Your son is hallucinating; he is having a psychotic break, and we need to hospitalize him immediately." Before I could respond, he took out a paper and pen and said, "I am going to send him over to the behavioral health facility. He needs to go right now. I will call, and they will be expecting him."

I asked the doctor, "What happened? What did he say during the few minutes I left him with you?" He spoke over me, insisting that I was in denial and that my son needed medication because he was mentally ill. I felt sick; the room was spinning, and I was speechless. My mouth was wide open, but nothing came out. When I finally found my voice, I said, "Sir, you must be mistaken. My son is not having a psychotic break; he is not mentally ill. He was recently diagnosed with autism, not psychosis."

I asked the physician, "What did he say?" He told me my son claimed to hear voices and see things. I looked over at Taalib and asked, "What voices do you hear?" He couldn't find the words to express it, but I knew something was amiss. Less than 30 minutes ago, we had driven here just fine. We talked in the car and stopped to eat, and he wasn't seeing or hearing things.

My mind couldn't comprehend why this doctor would make such claims, especially since my son had been diagnosed by two different psychiatrists who confirmed he was on the autism spectrum. This experience made me realize that many doctors may not understand the nuances of autism. I was furious and couldn't get out of my chair fast enough. I stood up and told this misguided, delusional, and ignorant doctor, "GOODBYE!"

We left the doctor's office, and I couldn't understand why he seemed to be exaggerating. I began to question myself: Am I in denial? He is a professional with years of education, but why was he doing this? It felt like I was in a movie; none of this seemed real or made sense. Deep down, I sensed something was off.

I watched my son sitting quietly in the room, absorbed in his cell phone. I couldn't see it; I didn't notice a child having a psychotic break. Then, suddenly, my "mommy meter" went off. I said, "Get up, and live as fast as possible." One thing became clear: we were alone, and not everyone could be trusted. From that moment on, I realized I needed to be more cautious about whose hands my child was in.

We had sought assistance and therapy at so many different places, and I noticed they always wanted to separate us. Never again. From now on, we are a package deal— wherever he goes, I go too.

Part 16: Chaotic Summer

A few weeks passed, and I got the county psychiatrist to refill his prescriptions. I continued to give him the medications, even though the pediatrician in Chicago had told me that most children on the spectrum didn't need them; they primarily needed help with social skills and speech therapy. However, it was suggested to keep him on the medication to help him stay calm in school. Unfortunately, it wasn't working. I observed that he was a different person on these medications — more agitated and unpredictable.

One day, the kids in the neighborhood were picking on him. We tried talking to their parents, but it felt like talking to a wall. There was no response, and this certainly made parenting more challenging. We attempted to reason with him, but it was ineffective. I suddenly heard the door close while at home with my younger daughter. I turned to find he had run after the other kids out of the house and into the rain. I panicked, not having time to put my shoes on. I grabbed a jacket and chased after him.

He couldn't understand why we repeatedly told him not to fight or he wasn't allowed to defend himself. The look in his eyes frightened me; I had never seen that look before, and we couldn't calm him down. It was the ultimate meltdown, and he was unable to self-soothe. It felt like something else was controlling him. I know that sounds crazy, but it's true. When I looked at him — his face, his eyes, and the tone of his voice — he almost seemed possessed.

After a few moments, I heard a loud crash followed by a thump. He had punched a hole in the wall while screaming, "Nobody loves me! Nobody wants me around!"

We had many more episodes like this. During one of his meltdowns, the dog bit him to snap him out of it and stop him. I looked around the house, and we were all shocked when it happened. My other children looked terrified but felt sad for him; they did not know what to do. They thought the same thing I was: "What is happening?"

I started to cry. His dad and I were so confused. We did not recognize our son; our baby boy was in crisis, and we could do nothing but comfort him, talk to him, and assure him that we loved and cared for him.

It was too much for him—all the bullying, the kids in the neighborhood calling him names. Summer after summer, for years, it's been the same thing. This summer was the worst because he had lost all his friends. The last friend had stopped talking to him due to peer pressure, and the other kids began to tease him about their friendship.

One day, I allowed him to go outside and told his little sister to keep an eye on him. I was always nervous when he went out because of everything that was going on. Then I heard my daughter calling for me, "Mom, something's wrong with my brother!" I followed her outside, but we couldn't find him.

I approached the corner to the young men's apartment and knocked on their door, asking if Taalib was there. The guy who answered told me that he and the other young men were outside, then closed the door on us. As we turned to leave, I saw my son running toward us, chasing the young men at full speed. I quickly stepped before him, trying to prevent him from confronting them. He was in a rage, and I could barely understand what he was saying through his tears. It was complete chaos.

I looked at the young men; they seemed calm but annoyed. One of them said, "Ma'am, can you please get him? We don't want to deal with him. He got angry and attacked us, and now he just keeps following us!" My son had been with them before, but something was different today.

I asked what had happened, and he replied, "Mom, they jumped me, ripped my clothes, and spit on me!" The young men didn't deny ripping his clothes; they just avoided making eye contact with me and wouldn't answer any more of my questions. I struggled to hold my son back; he was so strong. I couldn't calm him down or get him to stop. I was exhausted and desperately needed some help.

I told my daughter to knock on the door where they lived. The guy opened the door and told the young men to come inside. There was so much going on, and it was so loud the neighbors came out and asked if they should call the police. I begged them not to. That was all I needed was for them to show up and kill everybody.

I called his father to inform him about the situation. I was exhausted, I wasn't strong enough to hold him back. Finally, we got him home, had him shower, and disposed of his ripped shirt. It took us hours to calm down and prevent him from returning outside. He was out for revenge, and in his anger, he added another hole in the wall before finally falling asleep. It took days and weeks for us to convince him that revenge was not the answer.

We found a social worker for him to speak with because we realized we couldn't handle everything independently; we needed help. I tried out several support groups for teens, but many required cash payments and did not accept insurance, which became an ongoing issue. Finding therapy options that accepted our insurance was also a challenge. To address this, I changed my medical insurance and my job to seek the best help available. As summer ended and school began again, we felt hopeful.

Part 17: The Bloody Battle

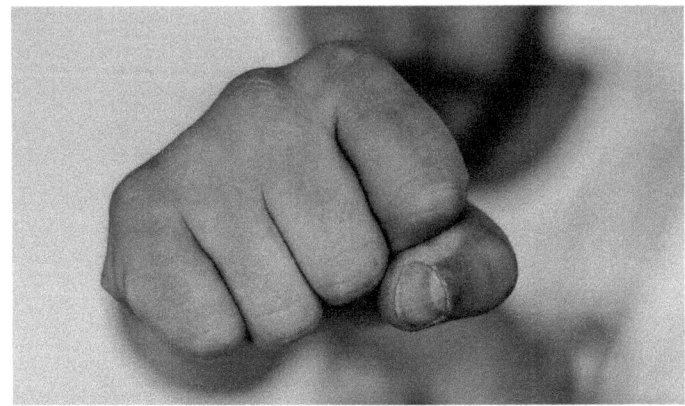

This was worse than the chaotic summer brawl. I received a call from the new school asking me to pick him up immediately due to a serious situation: he had been in a fight and had beaten a kid badly. The other boy had to go to the emergency room. Oh my God! My heart was pounding out of my chest.

When I arrived at the school, everyone was gathered in the office. They informed me that he had attacked a kid he claimed had been teasing him. After their investigation, it turned out that they had identified the wrong child. The boy he hit was not the one who had been bullying him; however, he was associated with the group that had been targeting Talib in the past. Talib had been hyper-focused on this issue because, according to him, the other kids wouldn't stop.

When I asked him why he had hit the kid, his response was, "They were bullying me with their friends and laughing at me when they jumped me in the locker room." This locker room incident occurred just a few months after school started, but Talib had not forgotten about it. Nothing had happened to the other kids involved. When they walked past him in the hallways, they would laugh and remind him of what they had done. Taalib felt that the adults were not doing enough to stop the teasing and bullying, so he decided to take matters into his own hands.

He was expelled for ten days and could not return until a physician and the school had cleared him. When Talib returned to school, some classes were rearranged to ensure that he and my son would not encounter each other in passing or in class. Unfortunately, that was just the beginning. The other boy's parents called the police and pressed assault charges against my son, which led to him being placed on one year of probation with regular monitoring by a probation officer. I was furious and overwhelmed with emotions, unable to comprehend the situation we were facing with my son. Every fear I had about how black men are treated in the judicial system flooded my mind, and I felt sick to my stomach. They didn't seem to care that my son had special needs or that he was on the autism spectrum.

I knew I had to make them understand that his impulsive behavior was unintentional. He was not a violent person, but he had endured enough bullying, teasing, and public humiliation. We explained everything to the probation officer, who informed us that the other child's parents wanted to take the matter to court and might seek restitution. I broke down in tears, showing him my son's diagnosis and detailing what Talib had experienced due to bullying, misdiagnosis, and medication changes. I recounted how, even at the 8th-grade graduation ceremony, that same kid had been annoying him while they waited in line to take the stage, taunting him about going to juvie.

This information came from the teacher's assistant (TA), who later stated that our son was not the instigator of the fight; instead, it was the other kids who had been harassing him. The probation officer relayed this information to the parents of the other child. With this new context, they rescinded the lawsuit on the condition that our son would write a letter of apology and stay out of trouble. Ultimately, they dropped the charges. However, this ordeal followed him into high school, and things did not improve.

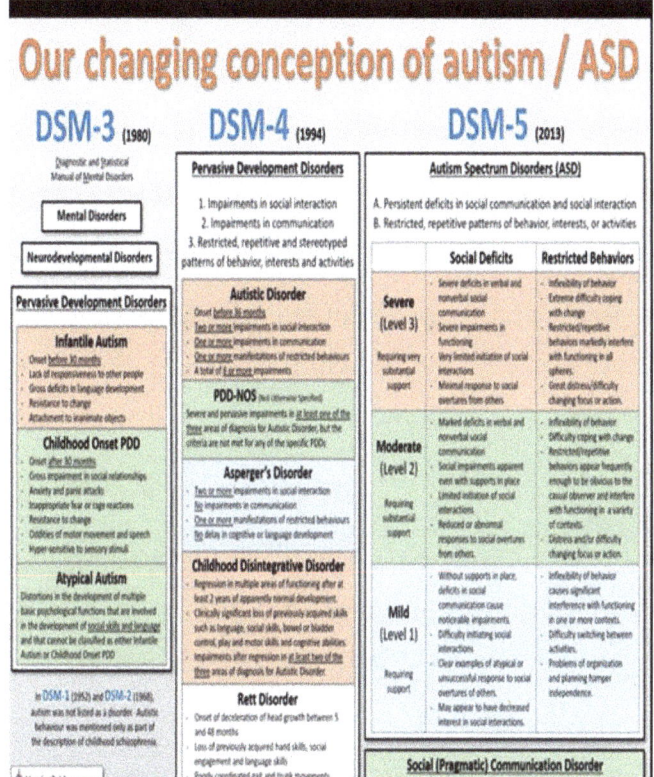

There have been seven significant changes in the understanding, definition, and recognition of autism:

1. The definition has evolved from a narrow focus to broader diagnostic criteria.

2. Autism is now recognized as a common condition, though it may still be underdiagnosed in women.

3. It is now recognized as a lifelong condition, rather than one that only affects children.

4. The view has shifted from seeing autism as a distinct category to understanding it as a spectrum with varying degrees.

5. Instead of considering autism as a single condition, there is no acknowledgment of multiple 'autisms,' recognizing its complexity and variability.

6. The focus has shifted away from 'pure' autism to an understanding that complexity and comorbidities are the norm.

7. Lastly, autism is no longer viewed solely as a 'developmental disorder'; it is now appreciated from a neurodiversity perspective, informed by participatory research methods. Authors: Francesca Happé, Uta Frith

Part 18: High School Days

High school was not the best time for him. During his freshman year, the same bullies from his past were all at the same school. At the IEP meeting, we placed him in a contained class, except during lunch. Along with the extra therapies, we requested a male teaching assistant (TA) because he didn't respond well to female staff. He was a big, strong young man, and we felt that if things got out of control, a female staff member might struggle to handle the situation. Additionally, we wanted him to have someone he could relate to as a young man. There were also safety reasons for having a male TA.

During the meeting, we discussed details such as transportation. We arranged for a van to pick him up and drop him off because, due to a few incidents on the general school bus, he could no longer use regular transportation without monitoring.

The school year started off rocky because of his probation, and the same young men, including the neighborhood bullies, attended the same school. Unfortunately, they wasted no time in starting their harassment, teasing him about his weight and other things. They laughed at his expense. He tried his best to ignore them, as we advised him to do, but it isn't easy to be laughed at in front of your peers.

We talked to him about it, but it was challenging to understand the full extent of the situation due to his difficulty in communicating effectively. Finally, we encouraged him to let us know whenever he was being harassed.

Even though they teased him, he wasn't helping the situation. The phone calls started almost immediately. Call after call reported that our son wouldn't follow directions, was wandering off, wouldn't sit down in class, kept going to the lunchroom without permission, and was swearing. Each call was always accompanied by an email. I told the school we needed to narrow things down: "Do not call us for things other teens are doing." This cut the calls down by half. However, he had been labeled as having behavior issues, so the calls only increased because now "bad" behavior was expected. It became hard for them to see him any other way.

One day, they called to say he was inappropriate, and a suspension was impending because they couldn't control him. An IEP meeting was called with the administrator, teachers, and dean.

We had to make more accommodation. During the meeting, we noticed he had Mountain Dew in one hand and a coffee in the other. I couldn't believe it! I said, "Maybe he wouldn't be as hyper if he didn't have so much caffeine." They agreed. As a result, he required two TAs and the teacher's assistance, but we had to wait until they could find another assistant to monitor his lunch and in-class activities. This was exhausting and mentally draining, but I knew I had to be his advocate, no matter what was happening or how I felt.

PART 19: Hitman and Gang signs

After a while, there were no more phone calls or emails, and things were relatively quiet at school. We still experienced a few issues at home, but nothing out of the ordinary. There was an incident on the bus where my son and another young man were talking about guns, but this situation was taken out of context. When I asked my son why he was discussing guns, he explained that they were talking about video games, and the bus driver agreed that this was what she had overheard. Nevertheless, Talib could no longer travel with the other children on the school bus; he could only ride alone in the van.

Another incident involved him drawing gang signs and talking about gangs. We noticed this behavior at home as well, and when we questioned him, he said he didn't know it was wrong to draw such things. However, I could tell that he was interested in this topic. We spoke with him and explained that gangs are not good examples to follow. Later, we discovered that the teacher had them reading about a Chicago hitman who had been assassinated at the age of 12. This material was inappropriate for children with special needs.

As I looked through the book, I was appalled and shocked. It discussed guns, murder, gangs, and gang symbols. Why would they have special needs children reading something like this out of all the books in the library? It took us months to get him to stop drawing and talking about gang culture.

We were learning a great deal about the school system, particularly the importance of asking questions and advocating for our children, as even educated adults sometimes do not make the best decisions.

Part 20: Weaning It!

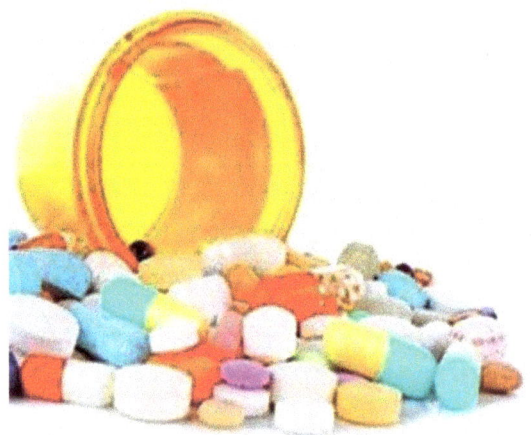

I made some changes to his diet and eating habits. We had made it to high school still on medication, but it didn't seem to be helping. It seemed to me that the medication was making him more manic, and not much changed for the better. He was still acting out, constantly agitated, and sometimes doing unexplainable things. However, we stayed on the medication as we were instructed. Eventually, I thought, "Something must change." So, we decided to try a new approach and wean him off the medication.

Many things just didn't seem right. I was baffled by how quickly he changed from a playful, loving child to an angry young man. The side effects were troubling: sleepless nights, gastrointestinal issues, and weight loss. We were doing our best as parents, but something wasn't right.

While all this was happening, I still had to care for myself. With lupus and diabetes, my health was not good, and everything we were going through wasn't helping. I continued my research for better health and came across a documentary called "The Gerson Miracle," which details the cure Dr. Max Gerson believed he had found for cancer and ways to avoid illnesses. Dr. Charlotte Gerson, his daughter, played a significant role in sharing his teachings.

As I dug deeper, I found a video featuring a man named Dr. Sebi (who was not a doctor but a master herbalist). He spoke about "electric foods" and explained how the body functions differently when it is in an alkaline state. Dr. Gerson and Dr. Sebi agreed that many of our illnesses today stem from what we eat. This idea was groundbreaking to me.

I began to reflect on my childhood food choices. We mostly ate at home, and fast food was not a regular part of our diet. One day, I watched a series of documentaries and a YouTube video about clean diets. They all conveyed a powerful message: food can prevent illness, harm us, or heal us. I decided it was time to apply this concept of clean eating to our lives. After all, what did we have to lose?

I changed our eating habits, started making fresh vegetable juices, and committed to regular detoxifications. I took him to my primary doctor for some tests, including blood work, to check for food allergies. Surprisingly, I discovered he was allergic to chicken, sesame, and coconuts. I was shocked to find that chicken was an allergen!

As I monitored his food intake, I also noticed that he had reactions to MSG and high-fructose corn syrup. After careful observation, I realized that his reactions included mood changes, sleeplessness at night, and gastrointestinal issues.

I started by eliminating certain foods from our diet and introducing more home-cooked meals. We discovered that he had some sensory issues with red sauce, food colors, and loud, continuous noises. He would bite and chew on everything. Our primary doctor also recommended adding a few vitamin supplements to our daily routine. Since the medications he was taking had too many serious side effects, we decided to wean him off all the medications. I remembered what the specialist said about children on the spectrum: the main challenges were speech, language, and social skills. That became our new focus. I knew we were going against the grain, but at this point, we were both fighting for our lives and our futures. It felt like we were at war with our minds, bodies, health, and spirit.

Part 21: Bathroom Boys

As we began this new journey at school, things remained the same. We had made it a habit to ask Talib how his day was and have him explain it in detail. We continued to stay in touch with the staff as much as possible. One day, the conversation took a scary turn. He told us that two boys followed him into the bathroom and were threatening to beat him up. We asked him if the teacher's assistant (TA) was present, and he said yes, "She was outside, and she made me come out." I had to think back to our IEP meeting; he wasn't supposed to have a female TA for this reason. That was it for me.

I called an IEP meeting and requested a transfer. There had been too much going on, and I felt it was necessary to have him in a controlled environment, at least temporarily. I made the request, but nothing happened. They rearranged his classes and found him another teaching assistant, but it was too late. All negotiations were off.

I contacted a child advocacy attorney and updated them on the current situation. The attorney reminded me of his rights in the state and informed me that they could move him and they would have to be responsible for paying for whatever school we chose. She also told me, "You will have to take drastic measures," and warned that "they won't like it. But you must do what is best for your child." She recommended writing a letter to Gebser. She explained that this letter must be typed and sent to the school administration, including the superintendent. It was a letter to put them on notice that they have a special needs child being mistreated.

I spoke to my family, and we developed a plan B in case we couldn't change school or if no action was taken. We contemplated everything we could, but we had all had enough of the bullying, the fights, the suspensions, and him being ignored by the staff and teachers for years. We had honestly had enough.

I wrote a letter filled with frustration and tears, reflecting on everything we had been through with him. I thought about how he had watched us struggle to understand things we couldn't explain. A few weeks after sending this letter, I received a call from the principal and the dean asking why I hadn't spoken to them before writing it. I felt terrible, but I had learned a great deal about how the system worked. I knew that if I didn't make a serious decision, we would be tossed around and re-planned repeatedly.

I had researched how our Black boys are at risk of being funneled into the school-to-prison pipeline; one more little Black child was all the system needed. My decision was not personal, and at that moment, I stopped worrying about whose feelings might be hurt. It was my son's life on the line, and I was determined to save him. After all, what choice did I have? We were his advocates; we were his warriors, and when it came down to it, it felt like war—either him or them.

My response to his question was, "It is not personal; my loyalty is to my son. I had to do what is best for him." I asked him, "Whom do you owe your loyalty to, my son, or your job?" At that moment, the dean understood, but I could hear in the principal's voice that he wasn't happy. But what could he do? He must know that he has to continue to do his job the way the system dictates, with no exceptions.

I understood his position. After all, he was a Black man, and I am sure he was already being scrutinized. I only know this because that is the life many Black people live, especially when they are the only ones in a position of power. We are watched, our abilities doubted, and our credentials questioned. I can only imagine that my actions, which he might perceive as a betrayal, didn't feel good or look good for him. I felt terrible about that, but I had to rescue my son, and that was all that mattered at that moment. We were out of time.

Part 22: The Tour

After the IEP meeting, amidst all the chaos, we received a call from the district coordinator. She informed us about three schools we could tour and potentially transfer to. One school was specifically designed for children with severe needs, the second was tiny, and the third, although somewhat distant, was larger and had an adequate staff. This third option was known as a therapeutic school. It provided hall monitors, security, and several teacher assistants, ensuring the children were consistently supervised.

We needed to find a safe environment for him while we worked on securing a better school for the future. And so, the process began again. After a few weeks, he was transferred to the chosen school, which was a 40-minute drive from our home. The bus picked him up each day. Although he wasn't thrilled about these changes, we explained to him that we needed to make a change and start anew.

Months went by, and things seemed to be okay. I started Taalib on a new diet: no meat, no high-fructose corn syrup, no MSG, and no fast food (except occasionally). It was a vegetarian diet with no soda or sugary juices. We ate home-cooked meals, mainly consisting of rice, vegetables, and fruit, and we made fresh juice. We also added several supplements to Taalib's diet to help alleviate his stomach issues, which included fiber with probiotics, melatonin to help calm him and regulate his sleep, magnesium to help calm him, vitamin D due to his low levels of omega-3 fatty acids, and a daily multivitamin.

I monitored what he listened to and watched on TV, avoiding anything violent. For the first few weeks, he didn't have a cell phone at school to minimize distractions. There were no phone calls about serious issues, no suspensions, just a few updates about his behavior. So far, the feedback has been limited to minor issues—he didn't want to participate in a class or would occasionally stand up and walk around.

Some adjustments were made to help him feel comfortable in his new environment. He was given extra free time, allowed to walk around if he completed his work, and behaved well. These privileges were earned through good behavior.

Part 23: New Day, New Diet

A few months passed, and school ended. Summer came and went without issues, but now we have summer school for a few weeks and 30 days of free time. We focused on our diets; he and I didn't just change what we ate; we also changed our mindset. We saw a therapist regularly and attended church for social skills, as many of the teen social groups were not suitable and often expensive. We talked about everything we could and homeschooled for 30 minutes per day during the summer. This new approach was going well; changing everything we were used to was challenging, but we had to adapt. There was no choice; it was a risk we needed to take.

After researching his supplements, I finally understood what he was missing and what he needed. Things got better and easier. Learning new recipes wasn't as hard as I had anticipated; many of the meals were similar, but we eliminated meat and avoided his sensitivity to red sauces and his allergic foods. For example, we used Alfredo sauce instead of marinara for pasta, and he opted for BBQ sauce instead of ketchup due to the color, not the sugar content. I also noticed his sleeping habits improved significantly, and his stomach pain subsided. His attitude also began to change; he became more tolerant of loud noises and people.

Now, our challenge will be getting the whole family involved in this new way of living.

Part 24: The Journey Continues

The Three Levels of Autism Spectrum Disorder

ASD Level 1

Requires Support: may have a hard time communicating with neurotypical peers.

ASD Level 2

Requires Substantial Support: may find it hard to communicate in a socially acceptable way.

ASD Level 3

Requires Very Substantial Support: may be entirely unable to mask and have very high burdens of self regulation.

It takes most people some time to understand what autism is, and some may never fully grasp it. It's not something we encounter every day; sometimes, people with autism are even nonverbal, which is not something we see regularly. I spent six years researching, consulting many doctors, and asking countless questions to truly understand it. People on the autism spectrum are not freaks or crazy; they are often misunderstood. They are human beings functioning on a different level. They will be the new adults of the future, so we need to get used to them. They have unique quirks and navigate the world differently, facing challenges with things many of us take for granted. They must learn to adjust to a world that can be unkind and perceive them as mentally disturbed, but there is much more to autism than that.

I am not a physician or a nurse; I am simply a mom who was desperate to find a way to help my son. This led me on another research journey. As I delved deeper, I discovered that autism is more than just a mental health issue; it is a neurological one. I learned that the pineal gland could become overloaded, triggering a chemical reaction that affects the blood-brain barrier. Much of this overload also causes problems with the stomach. Everything I found made perfect sense to me; it was logical. I decided to do what I could, hoping it would help my son. I was not looking for a cure, just a way for him to live his best life.

My research led me to videos, books, scientists, and other parents on the same journey to understand autism and its origins. I discovered that autism has been prevalent for at least 60 years. The statistics have changed dramatically over time: it was 1 in 10,000 in the 1970s, 1 in 500 in the 1980s, and currently, it is 1 in 49. It is predicted that by the year 2025, nearly every family will be affected by autism in some way.

I researched how autism affects children, with a particular focus on African American boys, where the statistics are notably higher.

Dr. Stephanie Seneff, an MD from MIT, researched glyphosate, a chemical commonly used to control weeds. She warns that if current practices do not change, the rates of autism could continue to rise.

As a result, many children will be impacted by autism and its associated challenges. The severity of these challenges can vary significantly; some children may be nonverbal, while others may have a mild learning disability and function higher on the spectrum.

Dr. Seneff regularly lectures on the topic, emphasizing her concerns that chemicals like glyphosate can cross the blood-brain barrier and negatively affect overall gut health. This is a pressing issue that requires our attention.

After conducting extensive research, I decided that I needed to begin detoxing everyone in my home. I also read a book by Dr. Umar Johnson, a child psychologist, titled "Psycho-Academic Holocaust: The Special Education and ADHD Wars Against Black

Boys". In his work as both a psychologist and a school principal, Dr. Johnson discovered that Black children are treated differently at every level of the educational system, particularly regarding suspensions. This disparity is even more pronounced for those with ADHD and ADD, especially among Black boys. The information I uncovered was astounding and readily available, but now I understand the importance of staying aware and vigilant about the school system. I feel empowered with the tools to advocate effectively for my son.

Part 25: The Research

I focused on reading and researching as much as I could every moment. I encountered overwhelming information, and I didn't know where to start. To make things easier, I focused on the more straightforward tasks, such as adhering to his modified diet and continuing with all the therapies.

His allergies included chicken, sesame, coconuts, red dye, MSG, and high fructose corn syrup. Most of these allergies seemed typical for chicken, which surprised me. I considered that chickens are often injected with hormones, so it might have been the chemicals used in their feed or cleaning processes that caused the reaction. However, the other allergies made sense.

As we continued with our new lifestyle, his stomach issues gradually improved. He no longer experienced constipation, and his bowel movements became regular. Previously, he had been so constipated that his bowel movements would entirely clog the toilet. Now, the shape of his stools returned to normal instead of the softball shape they had taken on due to chronic constipation. Months have passed since we adopted this new way of eating, and his condition keeps getting better.

I discovered that many of our children are exposed to high toxins from various sources such as herbicides, pesticides, and vaccinations. The pollution in the air we breathe and the food we consume is laden with harmful substances, which can feel overwhelming. In response, I started a detox regimen for my child, using a low level of detox lemon and lime waters along with juices. I also included essential vitamins and supplements that he was missing and made efforts to cut out sugars as much as possible. His diet consisted primarily of vegetarian options.

In addition to physical detoxification, I focused on mental and emotional well-being. We avoided any form of violence in media, practiced meditation, went for walks, and engaged in what I called "talk therapy." We made it a point to communicate with him constantly about a wide range of topics and offered daily encouragement. We were also very selective about who we allowed around him. Honesty was crucial; we made sure to tell him the truth about various matters because if he detected any dishonesty, it would cause him to become hyper-focused and anxious. Furthermore, we continued seeking therapeutic support outside of school for his mental and emotional needs, including hiring an ABA therapist to assist with day-to-day living skills.

Part 26: It is a Family Affair

Another year passed, and we ate less meat and detoxed; overall, our diet was going well. This lifestyle was different and challenging, but we remained steadfast in our pursuit. At home, things began to change as he was completely off medication. He faced a few issues at school, but they were quickly resolved.

We continued with all therapies outside of school, including speech therapy, and practiced our social skills at church. Promoting good behavior requires constant communication, redirection, and encouragement. We needed everyone's support, every family member, visitor to our home, and even every person or animal he encountered.

The patience required to handle day-to-day tasks was challenging for the average person. We always had to be aware of our surroundings, who would be present, and who we spoke to. Even standing in line at the grocery store became a teaching opportunity. This was a 24/7 commitment with no breaks; we had to be prepared for anything.

I became accustomed to the staring we received as I redirected him in different settings like the mall, school, or restaurant. I always explained to him, "I am not trying to embarrass you; I am on your side. I just need to teach you what you need to learn." We consistently spoke to and reassured him, ensuring he understood that we wanted the best for him. I also had to teach strangers and family members to be more accepting of my actions or at least understand their reasons.

It required constant communication, redirection, and encouragement of good behavior. To achieve this, we needed everyone on board: every family member, every visitor to our home, and every person or animal who interacted with him. The patience required to get through day-to-day life was arduous for the average person. We always had to know where we were going, who would be there, and whom we were talking to. Even standing in line at the grocery store turned into a teaching opportunity.

This was a 24/7 effort, with no breaks. We had to be prepared for everything. I even grew accustomed to how people would stare at us when I redirected him, whether we were at the mall, school, or a restaurant. I always explained to him, "I am not trying to embarrass you; I am on your side. I just need to teach you the things you need to learn." We consistently spoke to him, reassured him, and ensured he understood we wanted the best for him. I also had to teach strangers and family members to adopt the same attitude or be more accepting of the times I needed to step in.

I had to encourage his sisters and brother to get more involved. My oldest son seemed to have the most challenging time understanding autism and what it was. He was like most people who thought these behaviors had an intentional purpose and needed to be dealt with as if Talib were just another spoiled child. I didn't fault him for this mindset because it was very new to us in my community. We have not seen children with these sensory issues, quirks, and emotional disturbances. My oldest daughter sympathized immediately. She saw her little brother in need of help. My youngest daughter was confused about it; she didn't want anything to do with it initially but eventually came around.

As a family, we each found our way of coping with everything we were experiencing. It was something to which we weren't accustomed. My husband struggled with communicating with Talib, unsure of when to say, "boys will be boys" and when and how to discipline him. I felt overwhelmed by it all. Some nights, I couldn't sleep; I would lie awake thinking about what Talib was going through and cry.

When he was younger, a family member suggested he needed discipline, like a spanking, for his outrageous behavior. Deep down, I sensed that something else was going on. Out of frustration, I did spank him a few times, hoping to stop him from putting himself in danger, but he just looked at me and laughed. It didn't discourage him at all, and at that moment, I knew this was different. I never spanked him again.

When you have a child with challenges, you often face judgment from outsiders who look at you as if you are a bad parent, someone who can't control their child. Instead of offering help, they doubt your parenting abilities and believe they would handle things better. I was determined not to isolate Talib, so the people who loved us joined the fight alongside us. They wanted to learn how to support him.

Once, Talib had a sleepover at my sister's house while he was on medication. I had to provide her with a list of do's and don'ts: he can't eat certain things, he needs his meds at specific times, he shouldn't be left alone with small children or animals, and she must always pay close attention to him, among other things.

I told his baby sister, "You must look out for him and ensure he behaves." It felt unfair to place this responsibility on a little girl who just wanted to have a normal sleepover with her cousins. I felt like I was sending her a prisoner, and she was the warden. I considered changing my mind, but the kids were finally excited to see their cousins. I stayed until nightfall, but then my sister called. She said he was in a closed room and unsure what was happening. I could tell she was overwhelmed because dealing with autism is a lot, especially when it's not your child. So, I left, taking my children with me to get him. However, it was late, and we had a long drive ahead of us, so instead, we all stayed overnight with them and left the next day. Of course, I got no sleep.

This is hard. He can't go to sleepovers with relatives like the other children. It's not that I worry so much about the other kids; I'm more concerned about how he will be perceived and how others will behave around him. As time went on, things started to get better. We had been on a dietary plan for almost a year, and I could see him maturing into a different young man. The schools began to call and say he was visiting his classmates after finishing his assignments. We asked if they could challenge him more because he was getting bored; the work they were giving him had become too easy. They started to give him assignments at a higher grade level, but even that wasn't much of a challenge. Over time, this became the case in most subjects. He was actively participating in class, and his grades were excellent. He had outgrown the regular classwork; he started at a 4th-grade level, and now the school didn't have the capacity or staff to accommodate him. I requested that he transfer back to his home school and community.

We had a meeting to discuss transferring him back sooner rather than later. The meeting was split into two parts. The first was an IEP (Individualized Education Program) meeting. During the second meeting, they only briefly mentioned the transfer, so I had to interject, saying, "We're here to discuss the transfer, so can we get straight to it?"

The meeting didn't last long. The school said they didn't want him to leave, but they acknowledged there was nothing they could do. His community school wanted him back but had some concerns. After discussing these concerns with the teachers, counselors, social workers, speech therapists, and the school's transition administrators, both sides agreed he should return for half days.

This arrangement was beneficial for the community school and for us. It was closer to home and eliminated the 45-minute drive. Additionally, the school district was able to reclaim the funds for him since they were responsible for covering the costs of his therapeutic school.

Part 27: A New Plan

Our new plan to transfer him back to his community school was a step in the right direction. He was doing so much better. He had no issues at school and was calm, making good decisions. The plan was for him to attend both schools for half a day; in the first part of the day, he would go to the therapeutic school and then take the bus to the community school closer to home in the late afternoon. He was now a junior in high school and was about to face all his bullies and doubters, which made me anxious for him. However, I had confidence that it would all work out. We had worked so hard, and yet there was still more to do.

Before the transfer, there were constant conversations about what to expect, how he felt, and what to do if something came up. It was a consistent effort of encouragement and support. We reminded him, as we tell all our children, that if something happens or there is something he can't control, he should go to an adult immediately.

On the first day, it was a little confusing for him regarding where to go and what to do. He was excited, and I was invited to sit in the class. All his classmates remembered him, and they were excited to see him too. The teacher looked at me in shock, as if he couldn't believe this was the same kid. They were all amazed. He was engaging in conversation, making eye contact, laughing at a few jokes, and paying attention to things he hadn't done before. He was focused and sitting still in his seat.

I felt overwhelming happiness for him; he was finally getting to be with his peers. As the year ended, we had a new meeting to plan for a full transfer to his community school for a full day. I spoke to his former dean, who couldn't believe how far he had come. She had seen him at his worst and couldn't believe how much he had matured. It had been a long, tough road to get to where we were now.

Part 28: Senior Year

The year began like any other, and he decided to transition from a vegetarian diet to including fish. We continued to take our vitamins regularly, and he also started lifting weights and doing cardio. We temporarily ended the outside therapies, thinking we might revisit the idea later.

He attended two schools: a therapeutic school about 45 minutes from home and his community school. The therapeutic school operated on a part-time basis and, similar to the previous year, provided transportation to the main community high school.

The first few months were a bit rocky; it took some time for us to adjust, but overall, we were doing well. He made great progress and was able to join the wrestling team. He even had open lunch with his sister instead of eating in the classroom, which was fantastic. He was finally able to move around like other teenagers.

We connected closely with his teachers, the deans, and the therapist through emails and phone calls. Most of his team members were fully supportive, but sometimes, it took a while for everyone to get on board. As is often the case, one or two individuals struggled to comply with our team rules.

For example, one teacher used inappropriate language in her emails regarding our son. We corrected her immediately because certain words can trigger words, such as "disrespectful" and "aggressive." While it may seem minor, when working with a young Black man with special needs, such language can vilify him, which can be dangerous.

People who work with children on the spectrum understand that these children may sometimes appear disrespectful or rude because they do not comprehend situations like their peers do. It should always be a teaching moment where we help them understand if they are confused or unaware. Assuming they are being disrespectful on purpose is not acceptable.

Overall, his senior year was eventful. He had friends to socialize with, participated in sports, and achieved remarkable grades. At one point, they had to change his math class because he remarked, "This is too easy." He was also in a work-study program, which presented a few challenges—typical issues young men and women his age face, such as adherence to dress codes and following directions.

As his senior year progressed, we realized he would soon leave school and transition into adulthood. We understood that more work lay ahead, but we were committed to navigating it day by day, one step at a time.

Part 29: Undefeated

It's Talib's last year of high school and his last year as a student. Soon he will move into adulthood. We remember the journey that began not so long ago and the accomplishments that helped him get here. It was work, real work, and I know there will always be more work to do. But this journey shouldn't be as hard because now we understand what we are dealing with.

Every person on the autism spectrum is unique. While they may share similarities, no two individuals are exactly the same. It's important to find what works for you and your family. Establishing structure is key, and asking as many questions as possible is essential. Gather a support team around you, including family, friends, teachers, school staff, physicians, or anyone else who can help. Maintain open communication so that everyone is on the same page and ensure that they are listening to your concerns and are willing to assist you.

Take the time to read and research information that can improve your lives. Be patient, talk to other parents, join support groups, and read blogs to help alleviate feelings of isolation. Listen to your child. Don't assume that, just because you are an adult, you know everything—no one knows it all. Be prepared to learn from them, as this will facilitate better communication.

Understand your child's personality: know what makes them happy, sad, angry, or scared. Learn about their quirks, allergies, favorite foods, and sensory issues. Maintaining a positive mindset mentally, emotionally, and spiritually is crucial. Most importantly, while you care for them, don't forget to take care of yourself because your well-being is vital for their care. You are their advocate, and ultimately, you are responsible for ensuring they have a better life and future.

This journey can be challenging, and it's important to acknowledge that. However, you are your child's best advocate, and your efforts significantly influence their quality of life. The most important thing you can do is to... forget about what we commonly refer to as "normal" or what society considers "normal" and throw that notion out the window. Holding on to these ideas only leads to constant comparisons between our lives and those of others, which exposes us to unnecessary stress and judgment. I often remind Talib just to be himself and do his best because there is no definition of "normal." Everyone is unique and has their quirks.

As I write this book, we are still facing the challenges posed by a deadly pandemic that canceled Talib's graduation and senior dance, along with those of his peers. For almost two years, we have been quarantined at home and wearing masks everywhere. We used this time to learn to write, start new hobbies, and take online classes. We looked for ways to utilize our time efficiently. As a family, we are still navigating through it all and standing firm. I look at Talib with amazement because we have come so far, yet we still have a long way to go. We are hopeful for the future, aware that it will be challenging, but we know this fight is not over. As of now, we are UNDEFEATED! However, I understand there is more ahead, and the battle continues.

Part 30: What Happens After School Ends?

After graduation, all the pomp and circumstance are over. There is more. In certain states, support stops after 21 or 22 years. As a parent, you are on your own. It's as if they no longer exist, and you must surround yourself with parent organizations, friends, and family who will be your support. I found myself on Facebook, joining every autism group and googling as many organizations as I could find in my area, all for support and to connect with other people I could communicate with who would understand my experiences.

Part 31: Mr. Independent!

After high school, we enrolled in a program offered through the school district that continued Talib's therapies. During COVID, most of his classes were online and virtual. When the pandemic restrictions eased, he returned to in-person classes in a familiar setting where he knew most of his classmates. This program focused primarily on life skills and work training.

Once in-person classes resumed, transportation was provided by bus. However, Talib refused to ride, saying, "People are going to know I'm on the short bus." As a result, we drove him five days a week. Juggling work and transportation was challenging, but our family worked together to manage it. We successfully navigated this period.

Midway through the semester, Talib briefly worked at a pizza place, cleaning floors and taking out garbage. Unfortunately, this job ended poorly due to his difficulty focusing and following directions. His father had to pick him up, and while we were all disappointed, we understood that learning to work would take time. The boss, who had two autistic sons himself, was very understanding and allowed Talib to work as long as he could.

Similar situations occurred with subsequent jobs, as Talib struggled to maintain focus. We're still working towards the independence he desires, but we recognize the need to progress slowly and patiently. I even started my own business to demonstrate work processes and provide him with on-the-job training opportunities.

Our state offers assistance with on-the-job training, where support staff can accompany clients to their workplaces and provide step-by-step guidance. However, due to a long waitlist, we decided to take matters into our own hands.

It's eye-opening to realize how tasks that come easily to most can be challenging for others. Achieving independence will take time and patience, but we're committed to supporting Talib throughout this journey.

Despite being neurodiverse, Talib and others like him still desire independence in various aspects of life, such as working, driving, dating, and making new friends. However, some of these goals present unique challenges. For instance, in Illinois, obtaining a driver's license requires passing several tests or getting approval and a letter from a medical doctor.

We continue to face obstacles in our pursuit of independence, but we remain dedicated to helping Talib navigate these challenges and achieve his goals.

Part 32: So, what's next?

After high school, it is the end of all therapies and programs for most children but in our district, it will continue until he is 22 years old including behavioral, speech therapy, and occupational therapies some programs will also teach life skills where they will guide them through how to get a job, resume writing and cooking their meals. Some of these therapies can be taught at home, but it's essential to research what is offered in your area.

You can contact the Department of Rehabilitation Services (DORS) to find out what services are available in your area. In our area, there is a 5-year waitlist, and you can't get on this waitlist until the child is out of school. It is also essential to consult with local universities and colleges to explore programs and classes specifically designed for young adults on the spectrum and neurodiverse communities.

Therefore, you should start early and ask questions while they are still in school. Some private programs have high out-of-pocket costs, so be sure to apply for funding or scholarships. Many parents also must make the very sad decision to put their autistic adult in a group home or center for adult care for many reasons. However, it is essential to seek help when needed. As of now, Talib faces some challenges that we are still working through; he has days when he is sad and unsure of his future, and then he has days when he is okay. But never giving up and keeping your loved one safe is the goal.

Part 33: He Said "NO"

One day, Talib and I went to his doctor's appointment and had to use the ladies' room. When I came back, Talib went into the room without me. When I went in, the front desk receptionist wouldn't let me pass because of privacy. I told them he wouldn't be able to communicate with Talib properly, and they said they would ask him if it was okay to enter. They went and asked Talib, and he said no. They tried again, and once again, he said no. I was shocked he went through the whole visit without me; I had no idea what was said or done. It disappointed me because no one seemed to care, nor did the nurse or doctor come to ask me any questions about why we were there to see the doctor in the first place. It was all because of HIPAA, and I was not his POA, but that had to change fast. I recall speaking with a coworker a few years ago when we discussed Talib graduating, and she advised me, "Make sure you get POA or guardianship." Life passed so fast after graduation, and after COVID-19, I had forgotten, but this day sobered me up quickly. I got a POA immediately.

As our neurodiverse loved ones get older, they cannot speak or make decisions for life or their health. Many will need a medical POA set in place to receive information about their health and may also need a HIPAA waiver for privacy reasons. I learned all this the hard way.

Part 34: Stand on their own!

As parents, we often don't think about what comes next as we move from one day to the next. For those of us who worry about what will happen to our autistic or disabled loved ones when we are no longer able to protect them, it's essential to consider how we can ensure they are cared for or placed in a position to care for themselves.

Many families are willing to take on the responsibility of ensuring our children are in safe hands when we can no longer physically care for them. This is a blessing, but not everyone has that option. Some loved ones may need to enter assisted living facilities, group homes, or other living arrangements. This highlights the importance of having a trust, a will, a living will, and a DNR (Do Not Resuscitate) letter. Although it's difficult to discuss, we must be prepared and ensure that arrangements are in place just in case.

I hope that many of us can help our loved ones attain a level of independence with minimal assistance. As I updated this letter, my son has experienced some regressive issues, becoming almost entirely dependent on those around him. The stress of the world post-COVID has deeply affected him. The lack of social interaction has taken a toll on him, and we often find him in a dark place, engaging in self-talk with limited social moments with family and friends. He has no friends to call, and he's no longer playing his video games. I frequently check up on him, concerned about his well-being.

For some of our loved ones, living independently within a facility may ultimately be more beneficial, even if it feels heartbreaking. They will receive the comprehensive support they need, which may exceed what we can provide at home. It's something important to consider as we think about what's best for them and our families.

Part 35: Cutting with Conversation

I've realized that I need to be more intentional about spending time with Talib as he ages. It's easy to let our attention drift since he's no longer in school and has fewer external demands. He's starting to show more independence, which led me to cut his hair and engage him in conversation. When he was younger, getting him to sit still was the only challenge—getting his hair cut was never an issue.

As I cut his hair, I talked to him about his goals, asked about his day, and used this time to offer advice and guidance. Setting aside dedicated bonding time is so important, especially for our neurodivergent loved ones. These moments help strengthen our connection and provide them with the support they need as they navigate their world. Just because they're getting older doesn't mean they need us any less; in fact, our neurodiverse and autistic loved ones may need our support even more. Prioritizing this time allows us to foster trust and understanding, reinforcing that we are here for them as they grow.

Part 36: A Parent's Journey

The transition to adulthood presents unique challenges for young people with autism and their families. As our children grow older, we face complex realities that extend far beyond the structured environment of school.

My son Talib's journey into employment has highlighted some of these challenges. Despite efforts, including having a supportive manager at a pizza place and later in a warehouse position, he struggled to maintain employment. His difficulties in following directions and staying focused led to losing both jobs, causing him disappointment.

Additionally, his sensory sensitivities have intensified over time. He now prefers to spend hours alone in the darkness, engaging in self-talk (scripting) without any external stimulation—no television, video games, or lights. Medical care has also become increasingly difficult, as he refuses doctor visits and any form of medication or supplements.

The pursuit of independence has brought new complications. After accessing his disability benefits through a bank account, Talib began ordering food delivery services independently. While this shows initiative, it has made it impossible for me to monitor his diet, and his sugar craving has increased dramatically. Watching his younger sister achieve typical milestones—such as driving, socializing, and attending college—clearly affects him, although he tries to maintain a positive attitude.

The current situation is more challenging than his school years ever were. His push for independence, while natural, often manifests in ways that complicate his learning of life skills. As his only advocate and protector, I recognize that this journey requires tremendous patience, especially through broken windows, holes in the walls, and sleepless nights. Every day presents a different challenge, and we can easily become exhausted. There have been nights when he has slept, but he is constantly scripting day and night. Even in public, his lack of focus has become increasingly difficult to manage.

We remain hopeful and will make the best decision for him and our family. Though it is exhausting and sometimes disheartening, I remain committed to supporting him through these challenges.

The road ahead may be complex, but with time, understanding, and perseverance, we will continue to work towards helping him find his path while ensuring his safety and well-being in an often-challenging world. Yes, I sometimes cry when I think about how it must feel for him, but our journey will continue. Hard decisions will have to be made about how, where, and when, but we will take it one day at a time.

Part 37: I.E.P. Meetings and more info you should know

Never go alone! As emphasized in the book, it's essential not to attend an IEP meeting alone. Whenever there's a meeting or gathering concerning the care of your loved one, I strongly recommend bringing along a friend, family member, or someone you trust to help you process the information being discussed. Some organizations may also accompany you to these meetings. Reach out to child advocacy groups in your area or connect with other parents who may be interested in participating in these discussions; this not only benefits both parents but also fosters companionship and support.

Many meetings can move quickly, and they often use terminology that may be confusing. Having support can help you navigate this. Additionally, there are times when a therapist or psychiatrist may want to separate you from your loved one. In such cases, firmly say no;

never leave them alone with strangers. If they insist, ask why they can't address their questions in your presence. This approach is crucial for avoiding misunderstandings. If you absolutely must step out, request that the conversation be recorded. I've learned from experience that it's important to advocate for the presence of caregivers during these discussions.

What is an Individualized Education Program?

The Individualized Education Program (IEP) is a legal document developed under United States law for each U.S. public school child who needs special education. It is created through a team of the child's parent(s) and district personnel knowledgeable about the child's needs. IEPs must be reviewed annually to monitor the child's educational progress and ensure the achievement of established goals. The purpose of IEP meetings is to review, revise, and update your child's IEP regularly. How often do IEP meetings typically take place? The first IEP meeting must occur within 30 days of the start of the school year to determine if the child is eligible for special education. Parents or school personnel can call this meeting whenever there is a need to update or change something. Parents attending this meeting should have their personal goals for their child. Keep a pen and paper for notes for yourself, and keep copies of everything.

What is a HIPAA waiver?

A legal document that allows an individual's health information to be used or disclosed to a third party. The waiver is part of a series of patient-privacy measures outlined in the Health Insurance Portability and Accountability Act (HIPAA) of 1996

https://www.hhs.gov/hipaa/for-professionals/faq/authorizations/index.html

Americans with Disabilities Act –

The Americans with Disabilities Act (ADA) is a federal civil rights law prohibiting discrimination against people with disabilities in everyday activities. The ADA prohibits discrimination based on disability just as other civil rights laws prohibit discrimination based on race, color, sex, national origin, age, and religion. The ADA ensures that individuals with disabilities have the same opportunities as everyone else to access employment, purchase goods and services, and participate in state and local government programs.

https://www.autismspeaks.org/tool-kit-excerpt/what-are-my-rights-adult-autism

The Adult Autism Waiver (AAW)

is a 1915(c) Home and Community-Based Services (HCBS) Medicaid waiver designed to provide long-term services and support for community living tailored to the specific needs of adults with ASD age 21 or older. The program is designed to help adults with autism spectrum disorder participate in their communities in ways that suit them, based on their identified needs. Autism adult https://www.pa.gov/en/agencies/dhs/resourc es/intellectual-disabilities-autism/autism-services/adult-autism-waiver.html

POA -A power of attorney (POA)

A document legally authorizes one person (the "agent") to make decisions for another (the "principal"). The agent does not need legal training, and the principal retains the right to revoke this authority anytime.

Guardianship

It is a legal relationship created when the court appoints a guardian for an adult who has a disability and is not able to make or communicate safe decisions. Guardianship is a serious responsibility that requires the guardian to follow the law and court orders. Guardianship is not necessary if the individual is capable of executing powers of attorney. (Check with the state, different rules may apply)

The HIPAA Privacy Rule

-outlines key distinctions between consent and authorization, detailing when research waivers are required or exempted. It also specifies the rights and duties of both patients and covered entities. To clarify authorizations related to treatment, payment, healthcare operations, and research, consult the frequently asked questions section.

The Legal Rights of Autistic Adults, Guardianship, Supported Decision-Making, and Other Options

By Lisa Jo Rudy Updated on November 29, 2023

Medically reviewed by Steven Gans, MD

https://www.verywellhealth.com/legal-rights-of-autistic-adults

Driving license –

Illinois statutes prohibit issuing a permit to a person who has a physical or mental disability that may prevent them from safely operating a car unless that person can provide a verified written statement from a competent medical specialist stating that the disability will not cause the driver to be a danger to public safety. Drivers with disabilities must pass a theory test, which typically includes multiple-choice and perception skills sections, as well as a practical road test conducted by an instructor specializing in training for individuals with disabilities.

You should check with your state to determine the qualifications for drivers with disabilities.

CAN AUTISTIC PEOPLE DRIVE?

Many autistic and neurodivergent people can drive, but others cannot pass the necessary test. Each state has its own rules of the road for autistic, disabled, and even elderly drivers

Check the requirements for your state. In Talib's case, he passed the written test and the required course, but he does not possess the mental and cognitive abilities necessary to drive a car. Please verify your state's specific requirements.

Below is an article regarding driving for autistic people

Medically reviewed by Dannell Roberts, PhD, BCBA-D — Written by Kristeen Cherney on May 20, 2022, https://www.healthline.com/health/autism/can-autistic-people-drive

As we get older, we have to remember that our autistic children are still left alone; what do we do next? How do we plan a caretaker for them?

Here is an article that talks about what happens next after the parents of a child or adult pass away.

What Happens to Autistic Adults When Parents Die? By Claire Delano, BA

October 11, 2024, https://www.autismparentingmagazine.com/autistic-adults-when-parents-die/

Part 38: Tips and Other Info!

Here are some essential items and strategies that can help make daily life or travel easier when caring for a child or adult with special needs:

1. Backpack with Sensory Items and Snacks: Pack a well-stocked backpack, including sensory toys and snacks. It's also a good idea to have an extra one in the car for added convenience.

2. Organized Documentation: Use folders to organize important documents, or consider creating a digital folder on your phone or tablet to keep everything easily accessible.

3. Establish a Routine at Home: Create a consistent daily structure by setting specific times for activities such as bedtime and dinner.

4. Ensure Supervision Outside the Home: Always be aware of who your child is with when outside. It's important to avoid leaving them alone with strangers or unstable family members, even if they have pets.

5. Set Behavioral Expectations: Before family gatherings or events, discuss behavioral expectations with both your child and the other adults attending. Address potential sensory challenges, such as strobe lights, loud music, and crowded spaces.

6. Collaborative Support: Foster a comprehensive team effort among all individuals involved in caring for someone

with special needs or physical challenges, ensuring that everyone is aligned and working together effectively.

7. For those with nonverbal loved ones, it's crucial to pay close attention to their nonverbal physical and social cues, as they may not be able to communicate any issues verbally. Observing what they are not saying can provide essential insights; for instance, if they tilt their head to the side, it may indicate an earache. If they are holding their stomach, bent over, or sleeping in a fetal position, it might suggest stomach problems. Additionally, if they are squinting or bringing objects closer to their eyes more than usual, it's advisable to have their vision checked.

These nonverbal cues are crucial and can simplify life for both of you. It's recommended to schedule regular medical appointments, such as doctor visits every 6-8 months, which should include check-ups with the dentist and eye doctor as well. Waiting a full year for these visits may lead to unnecessary discomfort or pain for your loved one, and a year is a long time to struggle with health issues. Maintaining regular contact with healthcare professionals is ideal for their well-being.

RECIPES

Smoothies' tips

Frozen fruit works better than ice

And Almond milk/Cashew milk, coconut water/ milk taste better than just water alone

Because it is sweet. Many vitamins can be bought in capsules or powder form to add to smoothies. Nut-based chocolate milk has always been a winner in our house. I usually add fiber and probiotics to our chocolate milk.

You can always add extra fruit or vegetables to your smoothies, but remember to prep and

Cut up fruit and vegetables and place in freezer bags

(Double the zip lock bags if needed)

Detox water

2 lemons or limes, cut

Thumb size Ginger

Mint leaves for taste

And you could add a few leaves of cilantro (natural detox)

1 gallon of Distilled water or spring water

(the gallon should last a couple of days)

Vitamin water

2 or 3 tablespoons

of vitamins of your choice

(Many vitamins come in powder form)

Distilled, spring, or purified water

Ice cubes

Lemon or lime

And shake and place in the refrigerator

Chocolate smoothie

(all-in-one nutritional shake powder)

3 Frozen bananas

Coconut milk

Banana peanut butter smoothie

3 cut-up Frozen bananas

1 spoon of peanut butter or nut butter substitute

1 cup of Almond milk

Strawberry banana smoothie

2 cut-upFrozen bananas

Handful of frozen strawberries

1 cup of coconut water or water

Mean-Green Smoothies

A handful of frozen Kale

A handful of frozen bananas

1 cup of coconut water or water

Fresh Juices

The best juicer to use is a slow juicer or a masticating juicer

The use of fresh fruit and vegetables is recommended

Mean green juice and beet juice are my favorite juices to make because of their nutritional value and excellent benefits. I have learned to add a little cilantro to most juices to help with detox

But juice can also be made by taste; here are a few more juice recipes:

Green Juice "The Great"

2 green apples

4-5 leaves of kale

2 Cucumbers

Thumb-sized ginger

Half of a lemon or fresh lemon juice

You can always add a little water of your juice for consistency

Best Beet Juice

4 or 5 small beets

Half a lemon or lemon juice

Thumb-sized ginger root

2 cucumbers

1 apple

Sensational Citrus juice

6 oranges

2 lemons

2 grapefruits of your choice

2 apples

1 thumb-sized ginger

You can also mix it with sparkling water

Try Some Tea

Green teas

Cilantro tea

Gingo balboa tea

Mint tea

Golden milk tea

Ginger tea

Chamomile tea

Golden milk tea

Matcha tea

(Tea has great benefits)

You can always add a little water to your juice
for consistency

Holy moly guacamole

dip Ripe avocados

Red onion

Fresh cilantro (add an extra helping)

Fresh lime juice

Jalapeño (optional)?

Ground cumin

And sea salt

Part 39: Vitamins and Supplements

Please consult your physician before taking any new vitamins or medications.

In my research, I have found that the Western diet often causes us to miss essential nutrients and vitamins in our daily diet, and excessive sugar consumption leads to numerous other health problems. For many neurodiverse people, they are not just missing nutrients; they may have high heavy metal toxicity.

I recommend opting for fresh juices, smoothies, and green teas, and avoiding as many toxic foods as possible. I have also decided to add cilantro to my teas and incorporate regular detoxing.

Here is a list of foods to consider for individuals exposed to heavy metals and those who may be at risk of heavy metal contamination.

cilantro

garlic

wild blueberries

lemon water

spirulina

chlorella

Barley grass juice powder

Atlantic dulse

curry

green tea

tomatoes

probiotics

Also, if you aren't getting the recommended daily intake of vitamins, consider taking supplements.

Vitamin B, B-6, and C deficiencies are associated with poor tolerance of heavy metals and increased toxicity. Vitamin C has been reported to have chelating effects on iron. In one animal study, B-1 supplements were shown to decrease iron levels.

I also recommend the following due to many neurodiverse autistic people having stomach and sleep issues, and the following supplements may help.

Prebiotics

Probiotics

Fiber

Magnesium

Omega 3

Melatonin

Magnesium calm

What is heavy metal poisoning?

Heavy metal poisoning occurs when several heavy metals accumulate in the body. Environmental and industrial factors regularly expose you to high levels of heavy metals every day, whether from the lotions and soaps you use to the foods you eat or the air you breathe.

Current Version May 26, 2023

Written By Daniel Yetman Edited By Corie Osborn Medically Reviewed By Debra Sullivan, PhD, MSN, RN, CNE, COI Copy Edited By Kit Hitchcock

https://www.healthline.com/health/heavy-metal-detox

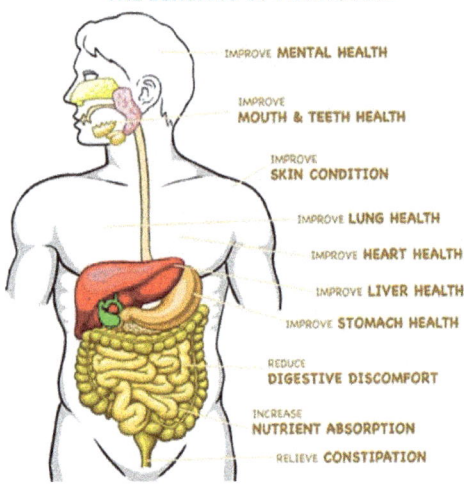

THE BENEFITS OF PROBIOTICS

IMPROVE **MENTAL HEALTH**

IMPROVE
MOUTH & TEETH HEALTH

IMPROVE
SKIN CONDITION

IMPROVE **LUNG HEALTH**

IMPROVE **HEART HEALTH**

IMPROVE **LIVER HEALTH**

IMPROVE **STOMACH HEALTH**

REDUCE
DIGESTIVE DISCOMFORT

INCREASE
NUTRIENT ABSORPTION

RELIEVE **CONSTIPATION**

Fundamental Benefits of Fiber

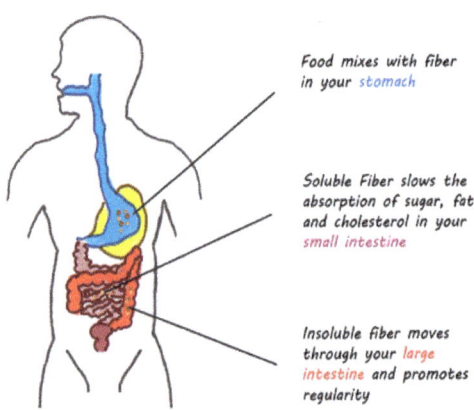

Food mixes with fiber in your *stomach*

Soluble Fiber slows the absorption of sugar, fat, and cholesterol in your *small intestine*

Insoluble fiber moves through your *large intestine* and promotes regularity

192

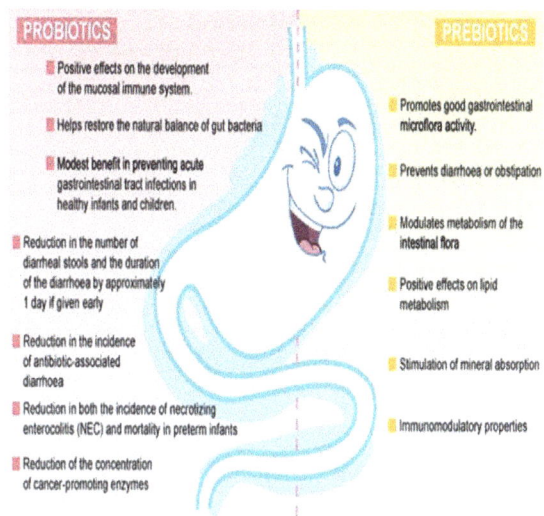

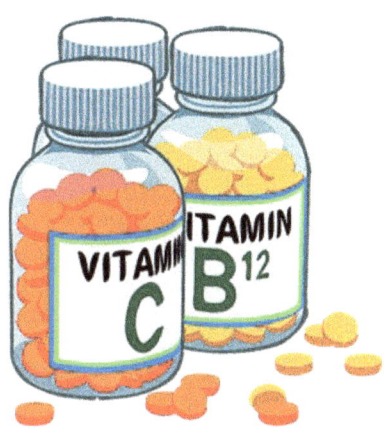

Supplements

Omega 3

Vitamin D3

Vitamin C

Vitamin B

Magnesium

CBD oil

Part 40: Therapies and Assistance

There are therapies and assistance for special needs, especially those diagnosed with autism spectrum disorder (ASD).

Here are a few:

Genetic testing

Stem cell therapy

Speech and language

ABA therapy

Group social skills

Child psychiatrist

Social worker

Behavioral intervention

Yoga and meditation

Eating disorders

and food Nutritionist

Definitions related to Autism

Individuals are sometimes referred to as being autistic or neurodivergent, although technically they can be any of the following-

Neurodivergent

is a nonmedical term that describes people whose brains develop or work differently for some reason. This means the person has different strengths and struggles compared to individuals whose brains develop or function more typically. While some people who are neurodivergent have medical conditions, it also happens to people where a condition or diagnosis hasn't been identified.

ADHD

Stands for attention deficit hyperactivity disorder. It is a medical condition. A person with ADHD has differences in brain development and brain activity that affect attention, the ability to sit still, and self-control. ADHD can affect a child at school, at home, and in friendships.

Autism

Autism is a developmental disorder with varying severity. It is characterized by difficulties in social interaction and communication, as well as restricted or repetitive patterns of thought and behavior.

Restrictive and Repetitive Behavior

Level 1: Individuals with autism often exhibit behaviors such as "being stuck" in various ways. This may include performing the same action repeatedly, continuously uttering the same phrase, insisting on following the same routines or rituals or obsessing over a favorite topic.

Autistic Disorder

This disorder is marked by impaired social interactions, verbal and nonverbal communication challenges, and unusual repetitive behaviors or significantly limited interests.

Asperger's Syndrome

Asperger's syndrome features fewer developmental delays compared to typical autism. It is primarily a social skills disorder accompanied by specific fixations. This condition is sometimes referred to as high-functioning autism.

Rett Syndrome

Rett syndrome primarily affects females, who are at higher risk for this condition. Girls with Rett syndrome typically develop in early infancy but then experience a slowdown in head growth. They lose previously acquired hand skills, struggle with social interactions, and exhibit Poor physical coordination, which can lead to severe overall impairments, affecting both expressive and receptive language skills, in addition to exhibiting symptoms typical of autism.

Applied Behavior Analysis

Applied Behavior Analysis (ABA), also known as behavioral engineering, is a scientific discipline focused on using empirical techniques based on learning principles to modify socially significant behavior. It is the applied form of behavior analysis; the other two forms are radical behaviorism and experimental behavior analysis.

Childhood Disintegrative Disorder

Also referred to as Heller's Disease, this condition is rarer than autism. In childhood, children typically develop for at least the first two years before experiencing regression, usually before the age of 10. In contrast, autism regression tends to begin between the first and second years of life.

Pervasive Developmental Disorder (PDD)

Pervasive Developmental Disorder is generally less severe than typical autism. It does not fit well within any specific category and is characterized by severe and widespread delays in development and challenges in social interaction.

Autism Characteristics

(Used to Diagnose Autism)

At least seven other disorders are closely related to Autism. Each disorder has symptoms commonly associated with autism, as well as its own unique symptoms.

Williams Syndrome

Fragile X Syndrome

Landau-Kleffner Syndrome

Prader-Willi Syndrome

Angelman Syndrome

Rett Syndrome

Tardive Dyskinesia

PANS/PANDAS, seizures, dental issues, sleep disturbances, and gastrointestinal symptoms.

https://pmc.ncbi.nlm.nih.gov/articles/PMC8 675523/

COMMON MEDICATIONS FOR ADD AND ADHD

Common Medications

Type of medication	Brand name	Generic Name	Duration
Short-acting amphetamine stimulants	Adderall	Mixed amphetamine salts	4 to 6 hours
	Dexedrine	Dextroamphetamine	4 to 6 hours
	Dextrostat	Dextroamphetamine	4 to 6 hours
Short-acting methylphenidate stimulants	Focalin	Dexmethylphenidate	4 to 6 hours
	Methylin	Methylphenidate (tablet, liquid, and chewable tablets)	3 to 5 hours
	Ritalin	Methylphenidate	3 to 5 hours
Intermediate-acting methylphenidate stimulants	Metadate CD	Extended-release methylphenidate	6 to 8 hours
	Ritalin LA	Extended-release Methylphenidate	6 to 8 hours
Long-acting amphetamine stimulants	Adderall-XR	Extended-release amphetamine	10 to 12 hours
	Dexedrine Spansule	Extended-release amphetamine	6+ hours
	Vyvanse	Lisdexamfetamine	10 to 12 hours
Long-acting methylphenidate stimulants	Concerta	Extended-release methylphenidate	10 to 12 hours
	Daytrana	Extended-release methylphenidate (skin patch)	11 to 12 hours
	Focalin XR	Extended-release deximethylphenidate	8 to 12 hours
	Quillivant XR	Extended-release methylphenidate (liquid)	10 to 12 hours
Long-acting non-stimulants	Intuniv	Guanfacine	24 hours
	Kapvay	Clonidine	12 hours
	Strattera	Atomoxetine	24 hours

Products are mentioned for informational purposes only and do not imply an endorsement by the American Academy of Pediatrics. Your doctor or pharmacist can provide you with important safety information for the products listed.

ALTERNATIVES

Research on CBD and cannabis has indicated that using small amounts of these substances can offer various benefits.

While a change in diet may be beneficial, it is not guaranteed to be practical, depending on the individual's physical situation. However, a change in diet, combined with an understanding of allergies and sensory issues, can be helpful.

Stem cell procedures have been gaining popularity in certain countries.

Ongoing research is being conducted to find ways to alleviate symptoms associated with autism, neurodiversity, and other neurological and behavioral issues.

You should always consult a doctor; this book does not intend to diagnose or provide medical advice.

Part 41: References, Links, and Websites

www.kidshealth.org

www.nationalautismassociation.org

www.autismspeaks.org

www.illinoislifespan.org

www.iancommunity.org

www.myaspergerschild.com

www.autismtreatmentcenter.org

www.autismparentingmagazine.com

www.autismspeaks.org

www.appliedabc.com

www.kidshealth.org

www.cdc.gov

www.autismspeaks.org

www.illinoislifespan.org

people.csail.mit.edu/seneff

www.drumarjohnson.com/#info

www.Autism.org

www.verywellhealth.com

Throughout history, several famous individuals have either been diagnosed with or rumored to be autistic or neurodiverse.

People on the autism spectrum live diverse lives, ranging from everyday individuals to scientists, actors, and musicians. Autism transcends boundaries, affecting individuals across various races and socioeconomic backgrounds. Below is a brief list of people known or believed to be on the autism spectrum.

Dan Aykroyd – Comedic Actor

Hans Christian Andersen – Children's Author

Benjamin Banneker – African American almanac author, surveyor, naturalist, and farmer

Susan Boyle – Singer

Tim Burton – Movie Director

Lewis Carroll – Author of "Alice in Wonderland"

Henry Cavendish – Scientist

Charles Darwin – Naturalist, Geologist, and Biologist

Emily Dickinson – Poet

Paul Dirac – Physicist

Albert Einstein – Scientist & Mathematician

Bobby Fischer – Chess Grandmaster

Bill Gates – Co-founder of Microsoft Corporation

Temple Grandin – Animal Scientist

Daryl Hannah – Actress & Environmental Activist

Thomas Jefferson – Early American Politician

Steve Jobs – Former CEO of Apple

James Joyce – Author of "Ulysses"

Alfred Kinsey – Sexologist & Biologist

Stanley Kubrick – Film Director

Barbara McClintock – Scientist and Cytogeneticist

Kanye West – Musician

Michelangelo – Sculptor, Painter, Architect, Poet

Wolfgang Amadeus Mozart – Classical Composer

Sir Isaac Newton – Mathematician, Astronomer, & Physicist

Jerry Seinfeld – Comedian

Satoshi Tajiri – Creator of Nintendo's Pokémon

Nikola Tesla – Inventor

Andy Warhol – Artist

Temple Gradin – Scientist

Ludwig Wittgenstein – Philosopher

William Butler Yeats – Poet

Wentworth Miller – Actor

Daryl Hannah – Actress

Anthony Hopkins – actor

Elon musk – tesla CEO

Sia – singer

Amanda Seals – actress

Always teach your children to be proud and love themselves

. - B. HADLEY (Dad)

About the Author

Elogeia Hadley

Elogeia is a devoted mother, caregiver, and advocate who is passionate about supporting families navigating the autism journey. A native of Chicago and a former medical assistant, she draws from her personal experience as the mother of a child on the autism spectrum to provide insight, encouragement, and practical support. Her work is grounded in love, resilience, and a profound understanding of the challenges and beauty that accompany caregiving.

Elogeia is also the founder of En'spired Publishing LLC and the author of several empowering titles, including Who Are We? The Truth About Black History: From Past to Present*, and *Rooted and Rising*. She is committed to self-care, mental wellness, and creating spaces where every voice, particularly those of children and caregivers, is heard and celebrated. Through her writing,

Elogeia continues to inspire hope, offer guidance, and uplift others with stories that reflect real-life experiences, compassion, and strength.

Every one of us is truly unique, and it's this individuality that makes us special—it's our greatest strength. Embracing our differences is what empowers us. Have you discovered what your unique superpower is?